THE JOURNEY OF THE ENGLISH-SPEAKING UNION

O friend unseen, unborn, unknown,
Student of our sweet English tongue,
Read out my words at night, alone:
I was a poet, I was young.

Since I can never see your face,
And never shake you by the hand,
I send my soul through time and space
To greet you. You will understand.

From 'To a Poet a Thousand Years Hence'
JAMES ELROY FLECKER (1884–1915)

THE JOURNEY OF THE ENGLISH-SPEAKING UNION

GERARD NOEL

MICHAEL RUSSELL

First published in Great Britain 2011
by Michael Russell (Publishing) Ltd
Wilby Hall, Wilby, Norwich NR16 2JP

Page makeup in Sabon by Waveney Typesetters
Wymondham, Norfolk
Printed in Great Britain by the MPG Books Group
Bodmin and King's Lynn

ISBN 978-0-85955-320-9

Contents

Author's Note and Acknowledgements

> I do not know what I may appear to the world, but to myself I seem to have been only like a boy playing on the sea-shore, and diverting myself in now and then finding a smoother pebble or a prettier shell than ordinary, whilst the great ocean of truth lay all undiscovered before me.

Thus did Sir Isaac Newton, father of classical science, acknowledge the inevitably partial nature of all that we attempt. That our efforts remain partial should in no way deter us. What matters is that we simply do the best we can.

Tentatively tracing *The Journey of the English-Speaking Union* has been a fascinating, yet humbling process. Always one is aware of the myriad people such as ESU staff, members, governors and supporters who, over the past ninety years, have given so unsparingly of themselves. If he were alive today, Sir Evelyn Wrench would be the first to acknowledge that it is only by their – often unsung – efforts that his vision has been able to come to such impressive fruition.

A great many people have helped in the writing of this book. My warmest thanks go to the following: HRH The Prince Philip, Duke of Edinburgh, President of the ESU, and the staff of Buckingham Palace, particularly Brigadier Sir Miles Hunt-Davis and Brigadier Archie Miller-Bakewell, Private Secretaries to His Royal Highness, Lieutenant-Commander Adrian Mundin, his Equerry, and Dame Ann Griffiths, his Archivist and Librarian. I must single out, too, Lady Soames, loyal supporter of the ESU and daughter of Sir Winston Churchill, former Vice-President and Chairman of the ESU; Anne de Courcy and David Burt, relatives of Sir Evelyn Wrench; past and present Chairmen of the ESU, particularly the Rt. Hon. The Lord Hunt of Wirral and the Rt. Hon. The Lord Watson of Richmond; past and present Governors of the ESU, particularly Mike Lake, Valerie Mitchell and Professor Alan Lee Williams; previous ESU staff, particularly Yvonne Theobald,

Cristel Guajardo and James Probert; and the present staff of Dartmouth House, who could not have been more welcoming.

Meriel Talbot and Annette Fisher were invaluable sources of information on matters national and international respectively. Gill Hale and Jeanne Huse were constant sources of support with archive material. Hanna Cevik kindly helped with photographic research.

I apologise in advance for anyone whose name I may have inadvertently omitted. Similarly any errors are entirely my own. Although I have tried to be as rigorous as possible, my viewpoint should not be taken as official ESU policy.

I would like to dedicate this book jointly to ESU staff, past and present, and to all ESU members, national and international. Their combined efforts have enabled the English-Speaking Union to make a unique contribution to world development.

Chipping Campden, 2010 GERARD NOEL

Foreword

HRH THE PRINCE PHILIP, DUKE OF EDINBURGH, KG, KT

I have had the privilege of being President of the English-Speaking Union of the Commonwealth since 1952. The world has changed dramatically since then, but, as this book makes clear, the English-Speaking Union has managed to adapt to these changes so that its purpose today is as relevant as ever.

This carefully researched book traces the evolution of a good idea into an invaluable contribution to international and intercultural understanding. I believe that Sir Evelyn Wrench would have been delighted to know that the Union has made this transition from a union of friendship among speakers of English into a dynamic body devoted to the promotion of the use of English as a medium of international communication.

No matter how good an idea may be, it cannot flourish without the dedicated commitment of loyal supporters. The English-Speaking Union has been fortunate to attract the interest of many influential citizens all over the world. It owes them all a great debt of gratitude for their continuing encouragement.

I would like to take this opportunity to offer my congratulations to the author and his helpers on their work in putting together this valuable and interesting account of a highly successful international voluntary friendship organisation.

Philip

Dedication

Readers of *The Journey of the English-Speaking Union* will find the footsteps of my father, Winston Churchill, virtually all the way through it. In January 1875, as a six-week-old baby, he was brought to live in Charles Street, not far from Dartmouth House, headquarters of the English-Speaking Union since 1927. In 1906 he was pleased to help Evelyn Wrench with letters of introduction for Wrench's first pivotal visit to America and Canada. Winston Churchill served both as Vice-President and as Chairman of the ESU. Of the ESU he wrote: 'The particular work in which you are engaged is marching hand in hand with the great destiny of our races in the world.'

In the Second World War my father played his part in helping to defend the world against the collapse of civilisation. At this time, the English-Speaking Union successfully changed its role, firstly to that of an aid organisation and then to a hospitality organisation. In October 1943 my mother, Mrs Churchill, made the official opening of an extension of the hospitality department. Readers of *The Journey of the English-Speaking Union* will note the tributes paid to the ESU in helping to alleviate the terrible distress suffered by so many at that time.

For my father, during the Second World War, English was not only a means of conveying a communal will to withstand barbarism, it might also, in happier times, become a language for all the world to use. As we now know, this has happened. A wave of globalisation has swept over all of us. The world has truly become a 'global village' and, of its own volition, it has freely chosen English as its communal language. My father would have been gratified.

The Winston Churchill Travelling Fellowships, the Churchill Lecture and the Churchill Medal commemorate almost fifty years of loyal friendship between Sir Winston Churchill and the English-Speaking Union. I know that, were he alive today, my father would applaud its illustrious past and fervently support its ambitious future.

MARY SOAMES

Introduction

On Friday, 28 June 1918, Evelyn Wrench invited fifteen distinguished friends to meet in a London club to discuss the formation of a new society. Six days later, on 4 July, the English-Speaking Union was officially launched. The choice of date can have been no accident. The Fourth of July is, of course, Independence Day, a federal holiday in the United States. It commemorates the Declaration of Independence in 1776, when the American colonies made a legal separation from Great Britain to create the United States of America.

The choice of 4 July can have been no accident. On that day in 1918 the First World War had lasted for almost four terrible years, with four more months remaining.

A generation of young men had been sacrificed. In Russia, the Tsar, his wife and their children would shortly be brutally murdered. A Bolshevik state had emerged; seventy years of vicious suppression of human rights would ensue. The world was utterly war-weary and in a state of acute political uncertainty. 4 July 1776 had seen a separation of two great democracies. Now Evelyn Wrench wanted to bring these two great democracies closer together. In so doing, he had an aim which was both practical and noble: lasting world peace.

The first issue of the ESU magazine *The Landmark*, published soon afterwards, in January 1919, outlined this core purpose of the English-Speaking Union (ESU):

> Believing that the peace of the world and the progress of mankind can be largely helped by the unity in purpose of the English-Speaking democracies, we pledge ourselves to promote by every means in our power a good understanding between the peoples of the USA and the British Commonwealth.

The wording of this declaration is as significant as the choosing of 4 July for the official launch of the ESU. The USA, the modern world's first superpower, has remained the dominant superpower throughout the twentieth century and beyond. In the USA's choice of English as its official language, there is a cultural debt to Great Britain. Evelyn Wrench is acknowledging the US as the dominant superpower, he is gently reminding us of this great gift of the English language and he is asking us to use it to promote mutual understanding between nations as the best means of avoiding the horror of war. All wars, even so-called minor ones, are bloody affairs. The First World War had witnessed carnage on a hitherto unprecedented scale; yet, if it became 'the war to end all wars', then something of lasting value would be salvaged.

Perhaps Wrench's aim can truly resonate only with those who have suffered personally from the ravages of war. For the rest of us, peace is the natural state of affairs. And yet peace can never be taken for granted. At the time of writing, the world has possessed chemical and biological weapons for over ninety years; poison gas was first used in the First World War. Nuclear weapons, with enough power to destroy civilisation forever, have lain in grim waiting for over sixty years. Tribalism with bows and arrows is one thing. Tribalism with chemical and biological weapons is quite another. Tribalism with nuclear weapons is unthinkable. In the early years of the twenty-first century, any reasonable-minded person would surely agree that, whatever our political differences may be, they are best solved by purely political means.

Evelyn Wrench was, above all else, a pragmatic man. (He was also, as we shall see, a visionary – but there is no reason why one cannot be both visionary and pragmatist.) In July 1918 it was clear that an end to the First World War depended on the combined efforts of the USA and the British Commonwealth. *Ipso facto*, the best chance of enduring peace seemed to lie in closer alignment between these two great bodies of people. Closer alignment requires better understanding. Improved discourse, via a common language, would pave the way to better understanding.

It must be emphasised that Wrench's intention was inclusive: '… Our sole and only aim will be to promote by every means in our power good fellowship between English-speaking peoples.' The first edition of *The Landmark* expressed the intention that the ESU would link up the sheep farmer in Australia with the New York businessman, and the gold miner in South Africa with the fruit grower in California. As a pragmatist, in 1918, Wrench viewed deeper understanding between the USA and the British Commonwealth as the best way forward at that time. Of course, as the visionary he was, nothing would have delighted him more than the truly global nature of the ESU today. For many nations and many diverse peoples, English is their second language. Indigenous language must always be cherished; it is the key to preserving our national cultures. But the world has freely chosen English as its international language. And English has become ever more important as a bridge between nations and peoples, particularly between those with fraught histories of political difference.

In wartime, understandably, peace is viewed as the absence of war. But peace is a vital concept in its own right. It is a necessary condition of economic, social and individual development. It is estimated that 800 million people go hungry each day. Out of a world population of 7.7 billion people, some 1.5 billion live on less than US$1 a day. The solution is not for 'rich' countries to become poorer. The solution is renewed emphasis on political, economic and social development to the degree that every person on this planet has a decent life. Clearly such progress cannot come about without shared understanding. The need for bridge-building is greater than ever. Ninety years after its inception, the relevance of the ESU is undiminished. Indeed it is heightened.

Our title 'The Journey of the English-Speaking Union' is as deliberate as was Evelyn Wrench's choice of 4 July for the ESU's birthday. For, above all else, the previous ninety years have been a journey: initially from the post-First World War reconstruction of a shattered Europe to the Wall Street Crash of 1929. When the hungry 1930s led to the near-collapse of civilisation in the Second World War, the ESU had a distinctive role to play. Afterwards Europe had to be reconstructed once again. Forty years of economic progress in the West saw the collapse of communism in the late 1980s. Thenceforth globalisation was inevitable. From the early 1990s to our own day, the ESU has risen to meet the challenge of a plethora of new countries emerging upon the world stage. Such countries require a warm welcome and a helping hand. Almost certainly, some of these countries will become key global political players. As such, they will inherit the moral and political obligation to preserve peace in an increasingly uncertain world.

If the previous ninety years have been a journey, they have also been a history. In fact, they have been many histories. From the outset, it was decided that the American ESU should be fully autonomous. Although the ESU, as originally based in London by Sir Evelyn Wrench, has had a close and enduring relationship with its American cousin, already we have two equally deserving histories. This posed an acute problem for the author. Would the best option be to dedicate half of this book to the history of the American ESU and the other half to the history of the UK ESU? Or would this tactic merely result in failure to do justice to either? After much deliberation and considerable regret, it was felt better to tackle only the history of the UK ESU, while fully accepting that there are long and honourable links with its sister organisation. Hopefully, one day soon, the history of the American ESU will be written. How fascinating it will be to lay out accounts of the two organisations, side by side, and compare them.

In fact we have histories of many ESUs in many different countries and in so many different branches of those countries. The ESU is an organisation founded by a man who was practical, noble, modest and dedicated. On its journey, it has attracted many others who have shared these qualities. The history of the ESU devolves into a multitude of histories. Ultimately these become the individual stories of those who have devoted so much of their lives to the ESU and its aims.

So a historian, grappling with the complexity of the ESU, is confronted by many histories, each deserving of further investigation. He is also confronted by practical concerns. No matter how meticulously records have been kept, most ninety-year organisations will have gaps. This is a fact of life. Dartmouth House, in London, the Headquarters of the ESU, was fortunate to survive the Blitz in the Second World War. However it is believed that in 1970, during the chaos of building work in Charles Street, certain of the records were lost forever. If so, they cannot be reconstructed.

On the positive side, ESU history is being unearthed. As this book was being written, the Alumni Officer at Dartmouth House discovered the existence of an extensive ESU exchange programme which had been run between the UK and Australia in the 1960s. It seems that there are hundreds more ESU alumni whose existence was hitherto unknown. Inevitably many will have become eminent in commerce, industry and the professions. We look forward to receiving all of them 'back into the fold'.

While a comprehensive history of the ESU is therefore impractical, this should not deter us from charting, albeit tentatively, a journey which has spanned the previous ninety years. It is tempting to begin at the beginning – on 4 July 1918. However, if we start somewhat *before* the beginning, perhaps the full richness of Sir Evelyn Wrench's world vision may be more deeply appreciated.

I
A Visionary Social Entrepreneur

'What was the meaning of life? Love was the key to the riddle – only the Eternal Verities counted ... I knew that in each one of us there was a spark of the Divine. That spark must be fanned into a flame.'
(Evelyn Wrench)

John Evelyn Leslie Wrench was born on 29 October 1882 in Brookeborough, County Fermanagh, in the province of Ulster, in what is now Northern Ireland. He came from a family of landed gentry. In *Struggle*, the second volume of his biography, he succinctly outlines both his family background and his early experience of two peoples separated culturally, economically and politically – despite speaking a common English language.

> From the date of his arrival in Ireland at the age of twenty-one, when he became a land-agent, my father identified himself with the landlord point of view. My parents represented the old landlord class. They loved Ireland, they were 'loyal' to Ireland as they conceived it ought to be – a feudal state in which the Protestant and property-owning class ran the country. Inter-marriage between Catholic and Protestant was frowned upon.

It must not be thought that Wrench's family were dilettante landlords; far from it.

> For over fifty years he [Wrench's father] lived in Ireland and no one could have worked more devotedly for its economic well-being ... When he was appointed an Irish Land Commissioner in 1887 his work took him to all parts of the country... Few Irishmen knew West and Southern Ireland as well as my father.

The work of the father had an early and lasting effect upon the life of the son.

> As a boy I was taken on some of my father's tours of inspection. I

> have vivid recollections of thirty or forty mile drives in outlying parts of Connemara, away from railways, seated sideways on an Irish car in drenching rain, wrapped up in a tarpaulin ...

Wrench freely acknowledges that 'The peasants had a grim struggle with nature in the wilds of the West ... I obtained my first realisation that life on the land was not the pleasant existence it is often pictured by town-dwellers.' His father spared no effort in his attempts to alleviate the farmers' lot.

> It was in search of new and up-to-date methods of agriculture and of suitable strains of livestock to improve the local Irish breeds that my father travelled through much of Europe. On these journeys he took his family and to these tours of investigation I owe my acquaintance with many out of the way parts of the Continent.
>
> No boy interested in life could have had a more stimulating childhood – a splendid training in tasks of administration and problems of government.

Already we may discern several fundamental imperatives in Wrench: altruism, practicality, a pronounced capacity for hard work and experience of other ways of living. All of these would later bear fruit with the foundation and management of the ESU. It would have been so easy for Wrench to have drifted along through an affluent, undemanding life. As he makes clear in *Uphill* and *Struggle*, his first two autobiographical volumes, his life was often far from easy. By deliberate choice, he dedicated himself to a hard, remorseless grind of overwork for one purpose – the betterment of humanity.

The Ulster of Wrench's youth was sharply divided by religion and class. As a member of the landed gentry, the Protestant religion and the ruling elite, one might expect Wrench to have held doctrinaire political views. Nothing could have been further from the truth. For there is another fundamental and, for the ESU, arguably even more important imperative Wrench took from his Irish upbringing: political and cultural tolerance. In his own words:

> Ireland has played such an important part in my life that it must have a section to itself. If any work that I have been able to do towards the promotion of unity among nations has been of value I owe it to my Irish upbringing. It taught me lessons about

> sectional antipathy that I have never forgotten. I made two separate attempts to help towards an Irish settlement in March 1917 and in August 1919. Neither attempt met with success but they gave me added knowledge of the difficulties and failed to shake my belief that the problem is solvable.

He freely admits, 'I do not know how much pure Irish blood runs in my veins, but it cannot be very much.'

> At most then I can claim to be one-eighth Irish and yet I frequently feel more Irish than English. Mother Ireland exercises a spell over her children that can never be shaken off. There is something in the atmosphere of Erin that makes Anglo-Saxons love her. Although I have lived in England for thirty-five years Ireland is my first love and I am still under her spell. I wish I could think that some day I might be called in to help in settling the age-long Anglo-Irish misunderstanding. In Ulster and in Southern Ireland I feel equally at home. When in the North I find myself trying to champion Southern Irishmen and in the South explaining my fellow Ulstermen ... Perhaps my upbringing in Fermanagh has enabled me to see 'the other fellow's standpoint' so wholeheartedly that sometimes I find that I am almost taking sides against myself. It is an uncomfortable state of affairs!

Wrench's political tolerance was matched by an amiability which ensured that he remained on good terms even with those who shared neither his views nor indeed his tolerance. For instance:

> The factor he [Wrench's father] failed to realise was that good government was no substitute for self-government and that control from ... London was unsatisfactory. If he had studied the history of the evolution of self-government in the British Dominions, as I sought to persuade him to do, he would have recognised that some form of home rule was inevitable.
>
> ... His whole life was devoted to practical tasks ... he and his colleagues were engaged upon the great work of enabling the poor Irish peasant to become his own landlord on favourable terms. [While he was doing this] other Irishmen were devoting their lives to the task of breaking away from 'England – their oppressor'.

Wrench's internationalism began early. Writing in the ESU's magazine

Concord, the renamed version of *The Landmark*, in the 1960s (when he had just turned eighty), the grand old man reminisced:

> Childish memories are not easy to recapture. I have tried to recall the first time I was conscious of the existence of North America without success. It is much easier to say that I do not remember a world without transatlantic associations. I spent the first four and a half years of my life ... in Fermanagh ... Members of our household staff and friends in the village would often refer to brothers or uncles or friends in the United States or Canada. I grew used to seeing letters with unfamiliar stamps; occasionally some 'celebrity' who had made good overseas, would return and revisit the scenes of his youth.

Summer holidays in Scotland whetted his curiosity further. 'The large steamers bound for North America passing down the Clyde ... were to me a source of never-failing delight ...' In Edinburgh, at the age of seven, he met his first two genuine Americans:

> Two American women staying there [at the hotel] were very kind to me and I regarded them with considerable awe. They told me of the land out west where a few years earlier redskins had been chasing bison on the plains – just as I had seen them doing in picture-books.

Several years later he met another pair of American ladies at another hotel – this time in Antwerp. He admitted, 'I was envious of their globe-trotting and could hardly believe they would ... be sailing back home to America in a few weeks' time.'

In 1896, at the age of fourteen, Wrench was sent to England's premier public school. 'Eton was a very wonderful place; I fell under its spell straight away ... the summer half ... was a succession of delights ... long afternoons on the river ... Henley Regatta.' Near Eton Wrench, a late-Victorian, was privileged on many occasions to view the most eminent Victorian of all. 'Yesterday I saw the Queen drive past. I got an awfully good view ... she looked very well and bowed to me.' To the fifteen-year-old boy, in 1897,

> an undreamt of era of splendour and expansion seemed to lie ahead of the British Empire. Why should we ever stop expanding? ... we were the people of destiny. It was evidently our job to run the world, and in running it Eton was going to play a big part.

With over 100 years of hindsight, it is difficult not to smile sadly at the good-hearted *naïveté* of this generation, many of whom would meet gruesome deaths in the mud of Flanders. Ironically, in 1898 the Wrench family went on holiday to Eastern Germany and Poland. For young Evelyn, it was a marvellous adventure.

> My appetite for foreign travel was purposely developed by my mother, who believed in its educational value for growing minds. To her I owe a great debt. At the age of 85 [in 1934] she still takes a keen interest in world affairs. I was allowed to do the negotiations with Cook's and to me were entrusted the money-bags. Could a boy of 15 or 16 have had a more delightful job than piloting his family round remote parts of Europe and the Near East?

'Germany was a paradise for a boy with a partiality for cakes and ice creams.' But in young Wrench, the Eton schoolboy, a social conscience was awakening. Typically his burgeoning internationalism invited comparisons between home and abroad:

> I had not seen many of our British slums in those days but I had seen enough to make me have an uncomfortable feeling that something was not right. I had been to the Eton Mission in Hackney Wick, I had seen the docks at Glasgow and Liverpool, and Dublin. I had become accustomed to seeing drunken women on public holidays. The men and women in the poorer districts in many of our big cities were slovenly. In Germany and Holland I never saw a beggar or an untidy person. I wondered how it was done.

The following year the family set out on another expedition, 'through Russia from St Petersburg to Moscow, across the Russian Steppes to the Caucasus, by boat to the Crimea, thence home via Constantinople, Asia Minor and Greece'. Once again, all of the preparations were made by Evelyn. As he proudly noted, 'No tour was ever more carefully planned.' They were going to see 'far-off places, away from the beaten track, far beyond the ministrations of Thomas Cook or Henry Lunn, [or] even Carl Baedeker ...'

In St Petersburg, 'Fabergé the jeweller had a world-wide reputation ... the Imperial Ballet was unsurpassed. The Russians were wonderful linguists; I greatly envied the ease with which they turned from one language to another.' Already Wrench had moved far beyond the cosy provincialism of Fermanagh.

> Another discovery I made in Russia was that the world was much more varied than I expected and that British influence was not as all-embracing as I had thought. Hitherto, when I had thought of the world it was a world in which, for the most part, Pax Britannica held sway. When I serenaded Queen Victoria in Diamond Jubilee year, two years before, I was taking my part in a tribute to the Victorian era and all it stood for, the expansion of the British Empire, the expansion of British industry. Anglo-Saxon civilisation was carrying all before it and must ultimately be worldwide. But in Russia, metaphorically speaking, I was pulled up with a bump. I was in a new civilisation, in a world-state nearly as large as the British Empire. And the Russian World Empire had this great advantage, its 8,000,000 square miles, equal in size to Canada, Australia, South Africa, New Zealand, Newfoundland and the Mother Country [Great Britain] rolled into one and more besides, was *contiguous* territory. It was one territorial unit. Ten thousand miles of ocean did not sunder its parts. In the Russian Empire I found a firmly established civilisation, with Slav culture, with a religion and literature entirely alien to ours, with an outlook on life as different from mine as chalk from cheese. Any thoughts I might have nursed of British ideals and culture sweeping all before them must be revised.

And there were other discoveries to be made. 'Wherever you went in city or village the churches were full. Wherever you went peasants were praying ... People were not ashamed of praying in the open ... Wherever we went we saw religious pilgrims.' Clearly Eastern Orthodox Christianity had its own validity. So, 'Why should Christians hate each other? In Ireland one section of Christ's followers abhorred the doctrines of the other. I had been taught that making the sign of the Cross and ritual were institutions of the evil one – but were they?'

Wrench's newly discovered religious tolerance was followed by something even more revelatory – something which would have the most profound influence upon his destiny. At a Russian Orthodox ceremony

> wonderfully robed priests and their assistants in the dim distance moved methodically about. Men's voices chanted in old Slavonic

> in a deep bass – of course I could not understand – but perhaps I did understand. The language they were using required no words, it was the eternal language of the Soul.
>
> As I stood there something in me was reaching out to unfathomable distances – I seemed to be stepping out of my body and the 'me' was engulfed in a great stream of light. I was piercing through the veil to Reality.

This 'piercing of the veil of illusion' is a familiar phenomenon to mystics. For the person experiencing it, quotidian existence can no longer be enough. Thereafter there will be a spiritual void. To have a sense of fulfilment, their life will need a higher purpose. Part of Evelyn Wrench's higher purpose would be the founding of the ESU. In 1899, as a young schoolboy of sixteen, he could have no way of knowing how painful his spiritual void would become – or how it would demolish a career of which few of his contemporaries could dream.

During the following year Wrench spent eight months in Germany learning the language. While there, his inquisitive mind alighted upon an idea which was both daring and innovative. In his own inimitable description:

> Postcards had played quite an important part in my life since I came abroad. Whenever I went, I wrote postcards to my friends. ... The German postcards were very well produced. I wondered how many picture postcards I had sent in the last eight months, certainly a couple of hundred. How many postcards were sold in Germany every year? If every German used as many postcards as I did, the total must run into several thousand millions – probably something like 4,000,000,000. The German postcard publishers must make a very good thing of it – how unenterprising English firms were, you hardly ever saw really good postcards in England. ... But then in Great Britain the sending through the post of a full-sized oblong postcard had only recently been made legal ...
>
> Would British people ever buy postcards like they did abroad? Why shouldn't they? British people when they were on the Continent bought postcards just like the 'natives'. Sooner or later the postcard craze would spread to England. Some enterprising firm would make a fortune in it. Lucky devils. How nice it would be to be rich and do what you wished and go where you wanted – but why shouldn't I be that lucky person? Absurd idea – a boy starting

> to sell postcards and trying to teach his elders to suck eggs – but why not? I was in Saxony, the country where most of the postcards in the world were printed. What luck! Why not find out all about it here? Why not?

I have quoted the previous passage in its entirety because it shows Wrench's infectious enthusiasm. What it does not show is his entrepreneurial flair. Many of us have 'brilliant' ideas; comparatively few of us put them into practice. But Wrench was a man who firmly believed in putting his ideas into practice. In the courtyard at Dartmouth House, headquarters of the ESU, his eulogy states simply: 'What Others Have Dreamed, He Has Done.' In founding the ESU (and other organisations), Evelyn Wrench was what we would now term a social entrepreneur. But long before, as a seventeen-year-old schoolboy, he became a commercial entrepreneur. And lessons learned in the harsh, unforgiving world of commerce served him well when he moved on to more altruistic aims.

Back in 1900, fired by ambition, the schoolboy Wrench mustered some start-up capital from his immediate family and returned to England. Beginning with just one employee, an Irish lad called Connolly, within three years he had built up a company with 100 staff selling 50,000,000 postcards per annum. He became what later generations would term a 'whiz kid', feted by the British and American press. Encomia soon appeared such as 'British boy wrests fortune from simple idea' and 'Wrench began on 250 dollars, now making 100,000 dollars a year'. With glee, Wrench noted: 'Requests for my autograph reached me from America. One correspondent addressed me "Mr. Evelyn Wrench, souvenir postcard king, London". The letter was delivered by the clever Post Office. I was flattered.'

Discovering a flair for publicity, Wrench promoted his business with stunts that would have made the great Phineus Barnum envious. Bringing out a special edition of twelve postcards dedicated to Captain R. F. Scott's first Antarctic expedition, he recalled:

> The last card posted before the Expedition left for Antarctic regions, portrayed a realistic Polar Bear. This was a bad *gaffe* – there are no bears at the South Pole. I ought to have known better. My mistake was pointed out in the Press. Never mind, free publicity was not to be despised. Till Captain Scott set out on his last voyage ten years later, we remained warm friends.

With the benefit of hindsight, the polar bear *gaffe* holds ominous implications. Although the young Wrench had older advisers, they seem to have been somewhat remiss in alerting him to business dangers. The postcard business became wildly successful, then *too* successful, an unbridled commercial monster. There were far too many product lines ('We had 10,000 different subjects in our series'), far too much stock, and far too much money tied up in stock. The gap between having to pay bills outstanding and receiving monies from debtors became a yawning chasm. Negative cash-flow killed Wrench's business as surely as it has killed untold numbers of businesses before and since. The world of the 'postcard king' came crashing down around his ears. Exhausted by overwork and beset by self-doubt, Wench lost control of the company upon which he had squandered so much dedication.

Six months before the collapse of the postcard business, Wrench had been introduced to the newspaper magnates Alfred and Harold Harmsworth, Lords Northcliffe and Rothermere respectively. Although Northcliffe's business advice came too late to save Wrench from commercial ruin, he was impressed enough to offer him a position as one of his 'bright young men'. Within a year, Wrench was assistant news editor of the *Daily Mail* then, a month later, at the still tender age of twenty-two, editor of the *Weekly Dispatch*. To mix metaphors, the latter was both poisoned chalice and revolving door for Northcliffe's 'bright young men'. After a mere four-month tenure, Wrench returned from holiday to find his successor blithely sitting in his editorial chair. Notwithstanding, Wrench's slightly bizarre apprenticeship with Northcliffe continued apace. He became the editor of the overseas edition of the *Daily Mail*. He was made a Director of *The World* and tersely told to 'buck it up', which he did. 'For the first time for 18 years *The World* circulation has stopped falling,' he confided to his diary.

> In 1906, my long cherished ambition was realised ... when Northcliffe was pleased with my work on *The World* I suggested that it was essential that the editor of the Overseas Edition of the *Daily Mail* should visit Canada and the United States. He agreed and gave me two months' leave of absence and said I might charge up a third of my expenses to the office. I could hardly sleep that night from excitement. I began collecting letters of introduction. [Winston Churchill was one sponsor.]

Wrench's visit to Canada and America was a pivotal event in his life;

as we shall see, with a direct consequence the founding of the ESU twelve years later. From his earliest days, Wrench had found travel invigorating. Nearly sixty years afterwards, he recalled, 'My first visit to the United States was a wonderful experience and in a lightning tour of seventeen days I travelled nearly 4,000 miles ... by train.'

'Europeans', he noted astutely, 'take their impressions of the United States from the Eastern seaboard, and they never penetrate further West than Chicago.' With admiration he recorded, 'Seattle was a wonderful place. It had boundless optimism, it vibrated with vitality ... Why shouldn't the citizens be optimistic?' Proceeding to Chicago, he found it 'a very wonderful city ... three things ... made a deep impression on me: its buoyant optimism, the hospitality of its citizens and its love of culture.' Of New York he wrote:

> Few visiting Englishmen can have ever received more kind hospitality or have crowded so much into such a short space as I did in those hectic hundred and twenty-five hours in New York. I was shown great department stores, the superb organising of one of the large banks, luxury restaurants and country clubs on Long Island; Chinatown – through which I was escorted by a friendly Irish-American Police captain, to meet grim figures notorious in the underworld ...

Overall, he concluded:

> As I sat in the libraries of my American friends and looked at the books by British authors on their shelves, and discussed world problems, I became convinced that the British and American nations must ultimately work together. They had a background of common tradition, common law, common literature, despite surface differences; there was an identity of outlook in many things which was fundamental.

One particular attribute of Americans impressed Wrench perhaps more than any other: their warm-hearted generosity.

> American hospitality should have a chapter to itself. It is wonderful. When the Englishman returns home he does not know how to requite the many kindnesses showered on him. In every town he visits he is made an honorary member of half-a-dozen clubs. What can he do for his American friends in London?

Wrench returned to London with, he freely admits, a broader view of life and an aim which would deepen inexorably over the following years. 'My chief interests now were trying to promote the unity of the British Empire, and to improve the relations between the British Empire and the United States.' But, 'My idea of starting an Empire Society had to be put away in my office drawer' where '... it remained for four years.' For, 'Now began six busy years when I started to climb the ladder of material success.' 'The Chief', i.e. Northcliffe, 'gradually switched me over to the business side [of journalism], where for six years I worked under Lord Rothermere ... I hardly knew how to fit all my jobs into the twenty-four hours.' The pressure was unrelenting. At one juncture Wrench confessed, 'This is the thirtieth day running that I have been at the office without a break.' Referring to his postcards episode, he noted wryly, 'When you have been a failure and have had a severe knock to your pride, you become sensitive. At first, you mistrust success; you wonder whether the pendulum of fortune will again swing away from you.' But year followed year, with ever-increasing levels of achievement. Gradually, 'My pride was soothed.'

And yet there were reservations as to how fulfilling materialism might be. Missing 'the greatest financial opportunity of my life' (a most generous offer by Northcliffe), Wrench casually remarks, 'Probably it was much better for me not to be a rich man.' Northcliffe was a capricious employer who '... certainly liked variety,' Wrench noted dryly. 'Although "the Chief" opened his heart to me, discussed his plans for the future and his difficulty in finding "generals" for his undertakings, and repeatedly told me that he hoped I would become one of the two or three key men in the business', Wrench had grave doubts. 'My stock remained high for another couple of years, but I think the high-water mark of my friendship with Northcliffe was reached at this time. My values changed ... I was no longer ready to give him that devotion to which he was accustomed.' Charitably he conceded, '... the fault was largely mine.' Wrench absorbed at least one vital lesson from 'the Chief'. 'Northcliffe possessed the power of concentration more than anyone I have ever met. Therein lay the key to his success.'

In 1908, on a second visit to the US, Wrench's health failed under the remorseless pressure of acute overwork. He was lucky to survive typhoid and a temperature of over 104. Undeterred, he returned the following year. 'A visit to San Francisco in 1909 was a very interesting experience. Such was the energy and enterprise of the inhabitants that, although it was only three years since the earthquake, an entirely new city had arisen.' Because this third visit is so important as a precursor to the setting up of the ESU, it is worth quoting the following passage in its entirety.

> In New York I met my friend Mr F. N. Doubleday [of publishing fame] and his partner, Dr Walter Hines Page, with whom I talked over my American experiences. I had caught the buoyancy and enthusiasm of the West and my American friends were pleased to find an Englishman glowing with enthusiasm for their country. American engineering prowess at Panama, American greatness in disaster at San Francisco, and American inventiveness, typified by the Wright brothers, had won my unbounded admiration. Our talk wandered to the cause of British-American discords. How could we achieve lasting friendship between our countries? There was woeful ignorance about the modern British Empire in the United States in 1909. Five years later Dr Page was United States Ambassador at the Court of St James['s]. In dark hours he acted as interpreter of one nation to the other.
>
> This was my third visit to the United States. I became henceforth increasingly interested in the relations of the two great sections of the English-speaking world, the British Commonwealth and the United States. Our destinies were bound together and the British and American peoples had a great part to play in the world. This conviction resulted in the founding of the English-Speaking Union nine years later.

In 1910 Wrench's life changed. Lord Northcliffe wanted him to become editor-in-chief of his newspaper empire. Lord Rothermere gave him a lucrative contract which assured his financial future. As Wrench put it, 'There was only one fly in the ointment. I no longer felt that the most important thing in the world, or rather in my world was to increase the sales of our publications.' The problem grew. 'I never could get the best out of myself unless I was convinced of the importance of my work. I began to have doubts – doubts whether I was making the best use of my life.' He chided himself, tried to stifle his doubts, and, as he put it, 'got on with the job'. But something was wrong – badly wrong.

On 6 May 1910 Queen Victoria's eldest son, King Edward VII, died. Attending his memorial service, Wrench was overcome by the occasion:

> The music at the Memorial Service in Westminster Abbey was wonderful. During the service Funeral Marches by Beethoven, Tchaikovsky, Mendelssohn, Purcell and Chopin were played. As I listened ... I seemed to hear the pent-up emotion of all who had suffered down the ages. The organ notes, soaring up to the roof, caught up my soul. I was shaken to the foundations of my being ... What was the meaning of life? Love was the key to the riddle – only the Eternal Verities counted.
>
> The scales fell from my eyes. I stood outside my former self, the business organiser, the careerist. Party allegiance fell from me like a worn-out garment. I vowed I would devote my life to great causes – to the Empire, to my fellows. From that moment my fate was decided. My days with Northcliffe were numbered.
>
> I saw in a flash the Divine conception of man. That each human being should be a temple of the Holy Spirit; I knew that in each one of us there was a spark of the Divine. That spark must be fanned into a flame. How could I have thought personal advancement was the goal for an immortal soul? In the presence of these immensities ambition left me. My ambition – in this atmosphere it withered like a plucked windflower.

As a sixteen-year-old boy in Russia, in 1898, Wrench had received his spiritual awakening with the 'piercing of the veil of illusion'. Twelve years later, at the service for King Edward VII, he received the same affirmation that generations of mystics have divined. Love was – and always will be – the key to the riddle. Nothing else works. It is our only salvation.

Wrench was a mystic. He was also a social entrepreneur. He didn't believe in navel-gazing. He believed in practicalities. Within four months, with no promotion budget or any other revenue, Wrench had founded The Overseas Club (now the Royal Over-Seas League), an organisation 'to draw together in the bond of comradeship the peoples now living under the folds of the British flag'. It was to be 'strictly non-party, non-sectarian and open to any British subject'. An article in the Overseas *Daily Mail* outlined the proposal. By 9 September there were 160 members. 'By the end of the year 12,000 people had applied for membership.' Unfortunately however, there was an Achilles heel. In starting the Overseas Club, while Wrench was still editor of the Overseas *Daily Mail*, he was laying himself open to the charge that the Club was, at least partially, a publicity stunt for the *Mail*. Worse, this is how Northcliffe regarded it. Wrench was scrupulously fair in pointing out that Northcliffe's motives were not merely commercial. 'The Chief' genuinely felt that the *Daily Mail* was the banner of Great Britain, and that what was good for the newspaper (increased circulation) was good for the country also. But Wrench admitted that, 'When people in the office talked about the Overseas Club as a "circulation stunt", I writhed. I vowed it would be no such thing.' Inevitably the rift between Wrench and Northcliffe deepened. 'I now realised that to him the Overseas Club was only a side-show. He did not understand that it was a "religion" to me.'

In 1912 Wrench and his sister Winifride made a world tour to promote the Overseas Club, visiting as many of the branches as they could *en route*. In Wrench's words:

> I wanted to unite these scattered centres. I wanted the Overseas Club to be a kind of 'Grown-up Boy Scouts', an organisation of human beings pledged to Empire service. The Empire was a living thing, not a mere political conception; it was the sum total of the human units that made it up. Each individual must feel that he was a link in the chain.

They visited Canada, Australia, New Zealand and South Africa. In each of these countries Wrench struggled to overcome the 'circulation stunt' *canard*. Speaking to a wide variety of audiences, occasionally hostile, in circumstances that were sometimes not so well arranged, certainly honed his skills as an orator. Travelling across the Pacific, after visiting the grave of Robert Louis Stevenson in Samoa, Wrench wrote:

> I suppose because it is at sea and I have time to think, I have several times lately been wondering what my future work will be when I get back to England. I cannot help feeling that the way will be shown to me, that somehow I shall be able to use all the experience I have gained directly in connection with the Empire.

Some time later, walking one morning in the Australian bush, '... my ideas were crystallising. The world-Empire to which I was ready to devote my life was a Commonwealth of free peoples ...' Travel had broadened his views; reflection had deepened them. Wrench was determined that 'such an Empire would not go the way of the Empires of the past ...' In South Africa, by 'the little thatched cottage where Rhodes died', Wrench remembered his last whisper, 'So little done, so much to do.'

On a dark, foggy November morning Wrench's ship crept up the Solent and he disembarked at Southampton. After the excitement of his world tour, he returned to a tiny back office in London. In his home country, his celebrity had vanished. 'I was just a young man with a "bee in his bonnet" who had chucked up excellent prospects for a fad ... I was prepared for hard times. I was ready to start at the bottom of the ladder again. But I had not reckoned with indifference.' And indifference proved a bitter pill to swallow. Wrench, the 'postcard king', the prospective editor-in-chief to the Northcliffe empire, was yesterday's man. Undaunted, he set about fund-raising, with marked success. Six months later, on Empire Day, 24 May 1914, the Lord Mayor of London and 'a great array of celebrities', including his old 'Chief', Northcliffe, opened a new headquarters in the Aldwych, central London. In Wrench's words, 'The Overseas Club never looked back.'

Shortly afterwards the First World War began. In *Struggle,* the second volume of his autobiography, Wrench reflected:

> The war divided the lives of my generation into two halves. 'Before the war was one era, 'after the war' was another. I had seen the last two decades of the nineteenth century. I had witnessed the passing of Victorianism. I had taken part in the hectic Edwardian years; 'pre-war' for me signifies youthful struggles, enthusiasms, ambitions, follies, failures, and successes. It was an age of growth in Empire-consciousness. It was an age of self-confidence in which we repeated 'God's in His Heaven; all's right with the world', and believed it. When King George came to the throne, an era of undreamt of prosperity and glory seemed ... to lie ahead.
>
> 'After the war' to me sums up great fervour, disillusionment and a new hope. Different values, a renewed consecration of purpose in a world in a state of flux. Gone is the easy assurance of pre-war days. There is a greater realisation of the complexity of life. But, as the years pass, a growing Faith.'

During the First World War the Overseas Club amalgamated with the Patriotic League of Britons Overseas to become the Overseas League. It collected the then tremendous sum of £1,000,000 for War funds. 180,000 associates bought the badge and pledged themselves to work for the aims of patriotism, comradeship and service to the British Empire, with 'no spirit of hostility to any other nation'. On Empire Day 1918 Robert Baden-Powell, founder of the Boy Scouts, declared:

> that he looked upon the Overseas League as an elder brother of the Boy Scouts' Association, and he hoped that one day they might be definitely affiliated as a junior branch. These two societies were born about the same time and were of equal numerical strength, were both Empire-wide and had much the same ideal and sympathies. The only difference was that one was for grown-ups and the other for the growing-ups.

Despite the massive success of the Overseas League, Wrench confessed that it was 'but a shadow of what I expected. I thought ... that I had started a movement as great as the [Boy] Scouts. Presumably I had over-estimated my gifts as an organiser.'

Wrench was being unfair to himself. His innovations in the First World War demonstrate his ability as an inspired 'ideas man' with formidable organising talents; these attributes are rarely found in the same person. The Overseas Tobacco Fund 'caught on like wild-fire' and gave solace to hundreds of thousands of men trapped in the trenches, with little comfort in their often tragically brief lives. The Overseas Aircraft Flotilla used the same idea of public donations, both in the UK and abroad, from civilians eager to do their bit for the war effort. With a quiet satisfaction, Wrench noted, 'Week by week until the end of the war we presented one or more aeroplanes to the Forces.' The Soldiers and Sailors' Fund resulted in hundreds of parcels being sent daily, together with much-needed medical supplies. Books were donated by the renowned publishing firm of Doubleday, Page & Co., New York, headed by Wrench's old friends, Frank Nelson Doubleday and Dr Walter Hines Page.

In February 1915 Wrench and Walter Hines Page had a meeting at the American embassy in Grosvenor Gardens. Wrench had always held Doubleday and Page in the highest regard. 'F. N. Doubleday, or "Effendi" as we called him, was one of my most intimate American friends ... The British Empire had no truer friend ...' Similarly, 'I rejoiced when Walter Hines Page was appointed as Ambassador at the Court of St James's.' For Wrench, Page, as well as being a cherished friend, was exactly the right man for the job. 'Few men felt the importance of a frank Anglo-American understanding more deeply than Page.' Page was one of 'a small but growing band that considered British-American co-operation essential to civilisation'.

Back in 1909, in New York, Dr Page, then editor of the *World's Week*, had asked Wrench how he found American feeling towards Great Britain. One of the themes which had come up in conversation was the limited experience which Americans often had of Britain, as part of a European tour. As Wrench put it:

> We agreed that one of the chief difficulties was that London's average American visitor stayed in a hotel and rarely saw the inside of a British home. In addition, few or none of our clubs extended their hospitality to visitors in the open-hearted way in force in the United States and Canada. During my three visits I had been deeply touched by the manner in which comparative strangers would ask me to their homes, and the extent to which in every large town I visited, I had enjoyed the temporary membership privileges of a chain of wonderful and luxurious clubs stretching across the continent.

The six years since 1909 had sped by, chiefly filled with Wrench's efforts on behalf of the Overseas League. But he had never forgotten the Americans' generosity to him and he vowed that he would repay it in a tangible form. If he could establish an Anglo-American centre in London, it would be a repayment and it would provide a bridge between two great democracies. When Wrench met with Page in February 1915, he mooted an idea for a new organisation, to be called the Overseas Club of America. (Three years later, this began life as the English-Speaking Union.) Page was delighted with the idea and replied, 'Once this darned war is over and I quit being a neutral, I will help you to get a million members for your show in the U.S.A. But while the war is on, my hands are tied.'

In 1915 the US had not yet entered the war. In his position as Ambassador, Page was unable to do anything practical. However it is impossible to overestimate the importance of this meeting. Page was a man of the highest integrity. He knew how deeply Wrench cared about Anglo-American understanding. There was no question that he was being merely polite. Wrench knew that Page was a man of his word. Most importantly for his peace of mind, he had received approval from the person whose opinion mattered most to him – an American uniquely positioned to survey the problem and its solution.

> From this talk with Page, I came away greatly heartened. Such was his sincerity that I was confident when asked to redeem his promise after the war, he would do so. I saw him several times during the war. Alas, he left England in October 1918, shortly after the founding of the English-Speaking Union, and died, worn out by his work, two months later. He was a man of great vision who regarded the greatest outcome of the First World War as the coming together of the English-speaking peoples and said, with rare foresight: 'For, if there be estrangement (between the British empire and the United States after the war), God pity the world.'

Together with Sir John Evelyn Wrench, Dr Walter Hines Page is the spiritual father of the ESU. In Dartmouth House, the London Headquarters of the ESU, his portrait hangs in the Revelstoke Room. It is impossible to gaze upon it without being deeply moved. Both men were idealists. Both men were supremely practical. Both men gave their lives for the cause of deeper international understanding. Dr Page's portrait is less than a minute's walk from Evelyn Wrench's simple yet profound encomium in the courtyard. In life, the two men were so close in spirit. It is fitting that their memorials are in such close proximity.

Wrench's key meeting with Page came in February 1915. Three months later, he was appointed by Lord Beaverbrook to act as Deputy to Lord Rothermere at the Ministry of Information. Wrench's job description was 'Controller for the Dominions and the United States, whenever Lord Rothermere is not available'. In fact, owing to Rothermere's unfortunate ill-health, Wrench had a more or less free hand. It was the ideal job for him, 'for it included the two causes to which I hoped to devote my life – the unity of the British Commonwealth and close co-operation between the English-speaking peoples.' It also meant that he was ideally positioned. 'My job gave me exceptional opportunities of meeting prominent Americans who happened to be in London during 1918.' With the entry of the United States into the war, the capital was flooded with important figures, as it would be again in the Second World War.

Wrench liaised with a wide variety of people, such as the leaders of the American Armed Forces, including General Pershing and Admiral Sims, war correspondents, editors, Senators, Congressmen, together with university presidents and professors. Nor were his meetings confined to Americans. In what he described as 'strenuous months', by 'associating with a cross-section of the American, Australian, Canadian, New Zealand and South African peoples I was at last in an atmosphere representing more or less the whole English-speaking world.'

Back in 1906, on his first transatlantic trip, Wrench had met in Quebec with Sir Wilfrid Laurier, then Premier of the Dominion. Laurier had challenged Wrench's Commonwealth concept of international unity. 'How can you leave out the United States?' he had asked. A grateful Wrench had reflected, 'Strange that it should be a French-Canadian who was the first to stimulate my vision of the unity of the "whole Anglokin" [the phrase comes from the Anglo-Saxon Chronicle].' Twelve years later, in his position as Controller for the Dominions and the United States, Wrench found that

> I did not label in my mind this man as an American or that one Australian; to me they were all members of the Anglo-Saxon community. What did it matter if the individual came from Melbourne or Milwaukee, Ulster or Utah? They were comrades in the joint crusade ... I agreed passionately with Walter Hines Page that the ending of the hundred and forty years' estrangement between the English-speaking nations was 'the most momentous fact in the history of either people'.

Wrench's meeting with Page had given him a sense of moral approval in his mission. His position of Controller had ideally positioned him. With the benefit of historical perspective, one can see that all of Wrench's life had been a necessary preparation. He had been brought up in an atmosphere of hard work and devout public service, with his father as an impressive role model. It is essential to remember that Wrench was a Victorian. He shared the Victorian spirit of enterprise and he shared the spirit of altruism that certain notable Victorians exemplified. Queen Victoria herself survived a tormented childhood and a lifetime of ill-health, punctuated by tragedy. Despite these setbacks, she restored the monarchy from its nadir to a 'golden age'. Through overwork, her husband, Prince Albert, literally gave his life for his adopted nation. Their second daughter, Princess Alice, was, like Wrench, both 'social entrepreneur' and visionary. She was also an early champion of professional nursing, as was her friend, the formidable Florence Nightingale, another visionary 'social entrepreneur'.

And yet Wrench, with his acute sensitivity and his warm empathy with others, of all races and social standing, is also a twentieth-century figure. From his earliest days, he had realised that people could speak the same language, yet be estranged. He had never taken his privileged status for granted, but had continually asked himself how to put it to best use for the betterment of others. As a young boy in Russia, he had received a spiritual awakening. As the 'postcard king', he had experienced great worldly success, followed by terrible failure. He had climbed to near the apex of the Northcliffe empire, before succumbing to disillusionment. In Westminster Abbey he had received his confirmation that service to others was his spiritual destiny, ranking immeasurably above commercial gain. With the Overseas League, he had founded an organisation of enduring worth to the Commonwealth, while gaining invaluable experience. Going one step further, creating a second organisation which would build a cultural bridge with America, was Wrench's masterstroke. He could help to repay Americans for their astonishing generosity. He could help to end the sad tale of 140 years of estrangement. He could build a cultural community for so many different people, from so many far-flung lands. And, most important of all, from the terrible carnage of the First World War he could salvage something of inestimable value – a cultural alliance for peace, for freedom. All his life had led to this decision. A lesser man would have flinched with self-doubt. Wrench went forward.

> Within a month of joining the Ministry I made up my mind that now was the time to launch the English-speaking brotherhood which had so long been occupying my thoughts. As early as 1908, on a railway journey to Philadelphia, I had hardly been able to sit still in the parlour-car because I so longed to be able to play a part in dispelling the fog of misunderstanding. I had waited ten years; never again would I be so favourably placed for starting the new society. It was my job to seek to improve British-American relations. I wanted our activities at the Ministry during that never-to-be-forgotten summer to leave lasting 'footprints in the sands of time'. Fate was helpful and I had several friends with whom I could discuss my ideas. It was in my diary of 12 June 1918 that I first referred to the new organisation as 'The English-Speaking Union'.

2

The Birth of the English-Speaking Union

'I told him about my English-Speaking Union and he was much interested ... As we were lying out in the garden we could hear the guns in Belgium ...'
(Evelyn Wrench)

On 28 June 1918 Evelyn Wrench invited fifteen friends (Appendix II) to meet in the sedate atmosphere of the private dining room of the Marlborough Club in London. All of them were sympathetic to the idea of forming a society to promote a better relationship between America, Britain and the Commonwealth. In fact one of the guests, Professor MacNeile Dixon, remarked, 'Why, it is such a very simple idea, I can't understand why no one else has done it before.' Professor Dixon was absolutely right; it was a very simple idea. A practical definition of genius is 'simplicity in retrospect'. The discoverer of the wheel was arguably the greatest genius in history; yet, once known, the invention seems patently obvious to the rest of us.

Irrespective of whether our best ideas are simple or complex, most of us never attempt to put them into action. Far easier to bask in the warm glow of elegant, theoretical solutions than to proffer those solutions to an often hostile world. However, as we have seen, Evelyn Wrench was made of much sterner stuff. By 1918 he had a wide and varied track record of putting practical ideas into action: his huge postcard business; his many innovations in the Northcliffe and Rothermere empires; the Overseas League; his wartime initiatives such as the Overseas Tobacco fund, the aircraft fund and the Soldiers and Sailors fund.

Nearly everyone who tries to put any new idea into action will quickly find out how hard it can be. Millions of patents get no further than the dusty shelves of technical libraries. In well-organised industries, 5% is a very good success rate indeed for new products winning significant market share. 'Social inventions', such as organisations, have a success rate that is probably much lower. For each famous society, such as the Boy Scouts, there are thousands of others which wither and die. Yet, some 130 years after Evelyn Wrench's birth both the Royal Over-Seas League and the English-Speaking Union go from strength to strength. Clearly Wrench was an innovator *extraordinaire*. He possessed many qualities which are usually mutually exclusive. He was both visionary and pragmatic. He could grasp both the big picture and the minutiae of detail. He was a superb salesman, yet meticulous in his business organisation. (Any manager of salespeople will confirm that paperwork is rarely their forte.) Although shy and self-effacing, he could be firm when required. And, despite intermittent bouts of self-doubt, he was extremely persistent. As President Calvin Coolidge astutely noted, so often in life, in the end, success comes down to dogged persistence.

However, the initial uptake of ideas depends upon one factor perhaps more than any other: timing. Victor Hugo once declared, 'There is no idea like the idea whose time has come.' As we have seen, in June 1918 Wrench was convinced that the time had come for his idea of bringing the Anglokin closer together. Now he faced the first hurdle. Seated at the large round table were representatives of England, Scotland, Ireland, Wales, Pennsylvania, Illinois, Iowa, Massachusetts, Victoria (Australia) and the British West Indies. John Buchan, the famous novelist, later Lord Tweedsmuir, was present. Boylston Beal, secretary to Dr Walter Hines Page, was present. The military was represented by Major Ian Hay Beith and the Church by the Revd W. F. Geikie-Cobb. The American media had its ambassador in Fullerton Waldo, of the *Philadelphia Ledger*. Sir George Sutton, Chairman of the Amalgamated Press, was present. Francis Powell, Chairman of the American Chamber of Commerce, was listening. In short, Wrench had assembled such a representative sample of interested parties as would put any present-day marketing guru's focus group to shame.

But what would his fifteen friends think of his idea? Wrench must have been on tenterhooks, although in *Struggle* he writes calmly, as though it were somehow predestined:

> After an excellent dinner the assembled company were in a receptive mood, and I outlined the scheme. The guests, in five-minute speeches, gave their views ... despite a knowledge of the difficulties, [they] were unanimous that the time was ripe for starting the movement. They promised their support.

Two days later, Wrench met with an ailing Lord Northcliffe. With typical generosity, Wrench recorded that

> he could not possibly have been nicer and we went out into the garden and ate strawberries and then lay on the grass and had a good all-round talk about the war. I told him about my English-Speaking Union and he was much interested and I think will help. As we were lying out in the garden we could hear the guns in Belgium every now and then!

How poignant to think of Wrench and Northcliffe discussing the ESU, an emblem of peace and tolerance, within earshot of the guns. Right up until the end, there was no respite for the front line troops across the Channel. With dreadful irony, Wilfred Owen's mother would receive the War Office telegram informing her of his death as the bells pealed out on Armistice Day. A generation of women would remain in solitude to rue what might have been, condemned to empty lives of loneliness. We, who take peace for granted, must never forget what the peace of 1918 had cost in human life. In the twenty-first century, where biological warfare is horrific and nuclear war unthinkable, the importance of the ESU has increased a hundredfold. Though the Belgian guns are long silent, the threats to world peace are more pernicious than ever. War is born of hate. Hate is born of lack of understanding. Only through celebrating diversity – and mutual understanding – can we possibly hope to survive.

A week later, on 7 July, Wrench reported:

> The E.-S.U. is going strong and I have enrolled over 50 members myself so far. We had our first Executive Committee meeting on Friday. We have taken as offices a nice top floor in Lennox House, Howard Street, a building about 50 yards away from the Ministry of Information and just on the other side of the Strand from the Overseas League. So my two shows are within 200 yards of each other.

Two weeks later, 'The present membership of the E.-S.U. is 130, so it is moving!' Not content with his own formidable talents at recruitment, Wrench was open to exploring other avenues of mutual benefit. Thus, 'On Thursday I lunched with a man called Hawkins who is secretary of the "Atlantic Union" to see if there was some way we could co-operate.'

As ever, Wrench was active upon many fronts. 'The first printed reference to the English-Speaking Union was in the *Daily Mail* on 10 July and the first reference in the American press was in the *Philadelphia Ledger*.' 'On Tuesday we had the second dinner of the E.-S.U. at the American Officers' club ... We have got some good Americans interested. I am doing a lot of spade work and all goes well.'

The 'spade work' was unrelenting:

> Then the New Zealand journalists arrived late on Friday night and I had to look after them yesterday and go to a lunch in their honour given by Beaverbrook. I have seen quite a lot of the latter and like him very much. The President of Cornell University is also over here and I have to look after him so you can see that there is not much time left over.

'Not much time' was probably masterly understatement. Let us not forget that this is the man who toiled, from dawn to dusk, for thirty consecutive days in the Northcliffe empire. There comes a point, though, when the stress of prolonged effort becomes more than flesh and blood can endure.

> For six weeks my enthusiasm was red-hot; all seemed plain sailing. Then came the inevitable reaction, perhaps accentuated by an attack of influenza. After nearly all moments of great elation in life there follows a period of flatness. It comes to all young organisations and is the testing time. Sometimes it lasts for weeks, sometimes for months. In the case of the English-Speaking Union it was of comparatively brief duration. I soon recaptured my initial fervour.

Wrench probably considered his mental exhaustion as nothing compared to what others had endured on the Western Front. But there are many types of struggle. As Winston Churchill would later demonstrate, words can be as important as bayonets when fighting for peace. Wrench was Victorian in his stern disposition to duty. Yet he was a man almost of our own time in the openness of his intellectual probing and his honesty about his emotions. His reflections on practical innovation are fascinating:

> I have often thought that starting new undertakings is comparatively easy. At the outset everything seems to be going well. The creator of the scheme is engulfed in his own enthusiasm and

generates further energy as he progresses. But frequently some extraneous circumstance or maybe ill-health brings him down to earth with a bang. He feels like a pricked balloon. In a detached manner he critically looks at his recent activities. How could he have felt such transports of emotion? But if his cause is destined to endure, the enthusiasm will return, and with it an abiding conviction that he is building on solid foundations.

By mid-October Wrench could report, 'I have had a tremendously busy week ... On Friday the big public lunch – 200 people present ... It was a tremendous success.' In the same week he met media Lords such as Northcliffe, Rothermere and Beaverbrook, politicians such as Winston Churchill and authors such as Conan Doyle and Arnold Bennett. In early November 'The E.-S.U. lunch on Thursday at the Criterion was a great success and we had 200 people there and Lord Robert Cecil took the Chair ...'

And then, finally, on 11 November, four years of hell were over.

It is impossible now [wrote Wrench] to recapture the intensity of feeling of Armistice Day, 1918. Although its coming had been expected, when the maroons sounded something seemed to snap inside us. Mixed emotions swept through me. Great gratitude for peace, an outburst of pent-up excitement, a sensation of participating in mass-consciousness, a feeling of uncertainty as to the future, an eager anticipation of a better world, a deep compassion for all who had suffered, and above all the lifting of a stupendous weight. The haunting fear – never admitted in words – that the forces of darkness might triumph and everything the English-speaking world stood for be swept away was banished once for all.

Understandably the aftermath of the First World War brought a sense of anti-climax. 'Many went through a period of acute depression soon after peace came. After the excitement of the closing weeks of war inevitable reaction set in. It was difficult to adjust oneself to the new and changed world.'

Meanwhile Wrench's fledgling organisation had growing pains:

Depressing news reached me from America concerning the English-Speaking Union. There were dissensions in the group that was organising the movement there, and I was asked to mark time. The knowledge that some of the American supporters of the Union were disunited was disturbing. How was it possible for there to be squabbling among workers for the cause of unity? Alas, I am now wiser. I no longer expect miracles. Some of the bitterest feuds I have witnessed have been in connection with work for international understanding.

Once again, mental anguish took its toll: 'I experienced a phase of acute depression. I lost faith in my scheme for the time being and in my ability to carry it through – though I am glad to say this lack of confidence was not of long duration.'

Wrench was soon to meet another charismatic figure suffering from spiritual exhaustion. Always he was concerned to alleviate suffering caused by political oppression and bring people of different outlooks together. It comes then as no surprise that, 'I was particularly interested in the Arab cause.' Eddie Winterton, an old Eton friend, told Wrench that he wanted him to meet a young archaeologist promoting the Arab cause. Winterton hoped that Wrench would introduce him to the Fleet Street barons, so that Arab hopes would get a fair hearing in the British Press. Amenable as ever, Wrench agreed, as he probably agreed to hundreds of similar requests for help that came his way.

One day I returned late from lunch ... In my outer office I saw an unassuming-looking young man, waiting to see me. He was shown in.

'I am the fellow Winterton asked you to see.'

I did not then remember very much about Winterton's friend. Let me see, he was the young archaeologist who was digging in the Middle East and got mixed up with the Arabs? Oh yes, I remembered now. He was the man about whom all sorts of rumours were floating round.

I looked at Lawrence. [T.E. Lawrence, 'Lawrence of Arabia'.] His eyes riveted my attention. They were the bluest I had ever seen. They seemed to be looking right through me to distant horizons. Despite his modest bearing, there was a dignity about Lawrence that compelled respect. He gave the impression that he would be equal to any emergency. I asked him to tell me why he cared so much about the proposed Arab State. It was a wonderful story he unfolded. He omitted all reference to the part he had played in the Arab Crusade. Only by degrees from brother officers, and above all from my friend Lowell Thomas, did I hear the fairy-like tale of the young Englishman, not yet out of his twenties, who had ... led hundreds of raids ... and who possessed an uncanny power over the wild soldiers of the desert.

Wrench had many further encounters with Lawrence and 'was able to introduce him to various newspaper friends'. He was at pains to point out that Lawrence 'wanted no publicity for himself, all he desired was that the Arab cause should be understood'. Entitled, 'With Allenby in Palestine', Lowell Thomas 'told the wonderful story of the Arabian campaign night after night at Covent Garden Opera House under the auspices of the English-Speaking Union.' Once again, Wrench was quietly instrumental. And yet for Wrench, as for all of us, Lawrence remained an enigma. 'Subsequent meetings only confirmed my first impressions. He was unlike any man I had ever met. I would never have dared to prophesy his future.' Sadly Lawrence's political disillusionment meant that 'he would just withdraw from the arena'.

Some years after the war, as I walked from the lift along the mosaic floor of the passage on the sixth floor at 87 Victoria Street to my flat one evening, I saw in the distance a small man in uniform. When I reached the door I wondered what a private in the Air Force wanted with me. The figure turned round and smiled, those blue eyes looked through me again.

'Hello, Lawrence!'

'No, Shaw please, Lawrence is dead.'

For all of his long life, one suspects, Wrench harboured acute political regret. He had proffered solutions to the Irish problem. He had done his best to help Lawrence get a fair hearing. The title of one of Wrench's later books, *I Loved Germany*, is bitterly poignant. How could he have known that, more than seventy years after its inception, the English-Speaking Union would 'go global' and act as a vital thread of mutual understanding in a world threatened with fragmentation and subsequent disintegration?

Back in 1918, however, the political landscape was changing and Wrench fully intended that the English-Speaking Union would be at the forefront of the new world order.

St Stephen's Day, 26 December 1918, will long be remembered as one of the landmarks in the history of the English-speaking world.

> It was an historic moment when President Wilson, the successor of George Washington, stepped on to the platform of Charing Cross railway station to be greeted by His Majesty King George V, the lineal descendant of George III. As I watched the two men shake hands and noted the warmth with which they greeted each other, I felt that history was being made before my eyes.

Accordingly Wrench wasted no time. 'It was a red-letter day when I had the privilege, as Chairman of the English-Speaking Union, of introducing a small deputation of the Central Committee to the President at the American Embassy at Grosvenor Gardens.' Wrench succinctly outlined the mission of the ESU.

> The English-Speaking Union, which has headquarters in Philadelphia and London, has been founded in no narrow attitude of race-pride, in no spirit of hostility to any people. It does not aim at formal alliances, nor has it anything to say to the relationships of Governments. It is simply a movement to draw together in the bonds of comradeship the English-speaking peoples of the world.

As *The Times* recorded, 'The President listened to the address with keen interest and evident pleasure.' And, as Wrench recalled, 'We then had a friendly and informal talk ... Mr Wilson wished us success in our efforts, and with a twinkle in his eye concluded by saying: "Just because we do speak the same language and can read each others' papers and what is said about us on the opposite side of the Atlantic, we should be very careful what we say about one another!"'

A few days later, on 5 January 1919, Wrench, with modest brevity, recorded another event of especial importance to the ESU.

> The following day I lunched with the secretary of the Atlantic Union and I am glad to say our amalgamation has taken place. That society was started in 1897 by Sir Walter Besant. It was founded when the German fleet attempted to seize Manila during the Spanish-American war. The British came to the assistance of the Americans and the Germans then withdrew.

Sir Walter Besant had asked A.C. Forster Boulton, former editor of the *London American*, to

> ... cooperate with him in forming a Society in London to entertain American visitors to England and enable them to see something

> more of English life than could be done by mere residence at hotels. I thought the idea was sound, but it should include the British Dominions; and in this way we formed the Atlantic Union which is now incorporated in the English-Speaking Union.

It is unfortunate that the records of the Atlantic Union are no longer with us, save one copy of the Annual Report for 1912. This affirmed that:

> The Atlantic Union is a Club or Society for the purpose of enabling visitors from the British Dominions beyond the seas, and the United States of North America, to acquire a more intimate knowledge of English people and their customs than it is possible to gain by a residence at an hotel or by casual visits to the ordinary places of interest. It is in no sense a political association, but it seeks to promote a better and kindlier spirit among the different branches of our race, by making the visits of our kinsmen to our shores partake more of a home-coming than the mere visit of a tourist to a foreign land.

In short, the objects of the Union were

1. To draw together the various English-speaking people.
2. To strengthen the bands of union by the formation of ties of personal friendship among individual members.

The methods were as follows:

1. Home Members who have the opportunity of offering hospitality and showing personal attention to visiting members are invited to do so.
2. The Union draws up every year a programme of social functions.
3. The Committee arranges for the introduction of visitors to members.

In 1912 the Atlantic Union numbered 400 members. It went on to do notable work. After the Dean of Canterbury joined its committee and invited a party to Canterbury

> ... similar invitations were given and carried out by the Deans of Rochester, Winchester and other cathedrals. The great public schools were eager to welcome visitors from overseas, and the Head Masters of Eton, Cheltenham, Wellington and other big schools showed what English hospitality could be.

In January 1919 the first issue of the ESU's journal, *The Landmark*, was issued. The original suggestion was to entitle it *E.S.U.* with the sub-title of *The Monthly Magazine of the English-Speaking Union.* However, the name was taken from a leading article in *The Times*, which had thus referred to the American–British spirit of cooperation in the First World War. 'This union bids fair to rank forever amongst the great historic landmarks in the moral and political history of mankind.' And, as we have seen earlier, Wrench had declared that the meeting between President Wilson and King George V in December 1918 'will long be remembered as one of the landmarks in the history of the English-speaking world'. So it seems that, certainly for Wrench, *The Landmark* had a particular resonance, signifying a new beginning.

The inaugural issue of *The Landmark* gave the aims, creeds and practical objects of the ESU as follows:

> The English-Speaking Union aims at increasing the knowledge of one another possessed by the English-Speaking Peoples. The ESU aims at no formal alliance, it has nothing to do with government, but is merely an attempt to promote good fellowship among the English-speaking democracies of the world.
>
> CREED
>
> Believing that the peace of the world and the progress of mankind can be largely helped by the unity of purpose of the English-speaking democracies, we pledge ourselves to promote, by every means in our power, a good understanding between the peoples of the United States of America and the British Commonwealth.
>
> MEMBERSHIP
>
> Open to citizens of the United States of America and British subjects. The English-Speaking Union is non-party, non-sectarian, and is open to men and women alike. It does not concern itself with the internal politics of the English-speaking peoples, and membership does not in any way conflict with the duties of good citizenship. It is realised that each member's first duty is to the land of his birth or adoption.
>
> PRACTICAL OBJECTS
>
> To establish ESUs wherever the English language is spoken, with

the view of promoting locally every movement which makes for the friendship of the English-speaking peoples.

To extend the hand of welcome in every country to English-speaking visitors.

To celebrate jointly such National Festivals as: Shakespeare's Birthday (23 April), Empire Day (24 May), Independence Day (4 July), Thanksgiving Day [then the last Thursday in November, now the fourth Tuesday in November.]

[Issue 3 of *The Landmark* recorded the following additions: Magna Carta Day (13 June), Washington's Birthday (22 February) and Armistice Day (11 November).]

To make English-speaking peoples better known to each other by the interchange of visits, by correspondence, by the printed word and lectures, by an interchange of professors and preachers, by sporting contests and by any other means.

To publish a magazine devoted to the cause of the English-Speaking Union.

To take every opportunity, through the press and otherwise, of emphasising the traditions and institutions possessed in common by the English-Speaking Union.

HEADQUARTERS

The headquarters of the English-Speaking Union to be in Washington, D.C. and London, England. [The first London location was Lennox House, Howard Street, Strand, overlooking the Australian Government building. In April 1920 new premises were secured on the third floor of Trafalgar Buildings, 1 Charing Cross.]

BRANCHES

Each individual English-Speaking Union is to be self-governing, and there will be no interference from headquarters so long as a branch carries on practical work tending to promote the spirit of comradeship between the English-speaking peoples.

The first issue of *The Landmark* gave the membership as already over 800. On average, over 100 members a month had been recruited – a testament to the vigour of Wrench and his comrades. The following month, in the second issue of *The Landmark*, the amalgamation of the ESU and the Atlantic Union was reported. As can be seen from the similarity of aims, there was an obvious synergy, with considerable benefits to both organisations.

The wording of the constitution is a tribute to Wrench's tact and diplomacy. The Americans are placed first. The holidays are arranged in order of date, so there can be no possible offence. The providers of financial expertise are thoroughly Establishment; the bankers are Coutts, the auditors are Price Waterhouse. The British President is the Rt. Hon. A. J. Balfour, OM and the American President is the Hon. Wm. H. Taft, the former US President. There are 30 Vice-Presidents (including Winston Churchill, Frank Doubleday, and the later US President, Franklin Roosevelt.) The General Committee numbers 26 persons (including John Buchan).

This first issue of *The Landmark* gave an illustration of a portrait of Dr Walter Hines Page – the same portrait that hangs today in Dartmouth House. The tribute accompanying this illustration (almost certainly written by Wrench) notes: 'His death, at the very moment of the realisation of his deepest aspirations for Anglo-American unity, terminated a very great career.' That inaugural issue of *The Landmark* begins with a message from Dr Page. It notes that '... in all free countries, governments are but instruments of the people's will, the people of the English-speaking world must be in agreement'. Referring to the *rapprochement* between the United States and Great Britain in the First World War, Dr Page adjudges that, 'To my thinking, this union of purpose and of effort in war is the most momentous fact in the history of either people.' And, in words which resonate across the intervening century, he declaims that 'this union of purpose'

> ... sets all tides flowing towards a permanent union of aim in world-affairs. But irritations and distractions are sure to come, as they always come in human dealings that involve large masses of men; and the generation that survives this war and the generations that follow will have the task to distinguish between mere irritations and estrangement. For, if there be estrangement, God pity the world!

That first issue of *The Landmark* had many notable articles, such as a transcript of a speech by the British president, Mr Balfour, entitled 'The Future of the World', and 'Materialism and Idealism in America' by Professor George Santayana. 'The Irish Nightmare' (probably also written by Wrench) asked:

> Cannot Mr Lloyd George, now that he is returned to power with such an enormous majority, devote his great talents and those of his Ministry to Ireland – no problem calls for more urgent attention. To bring order out of the present chaos would be the highest act of statesmanship. Bewilderingly difficult though the task may be, we believe it is capable of solution.

As Wrench wrote in the second issue of *The Landmark*:

> Our mailbag is a most interesting one, and we are always very pleased to receive letters from our world-wide membership. We hope that members will make a point of corresponding with one another and thus form links of friendship across the seas. Many wrote to express their approval of the ESU. 'I will always do all in my power to help your cause in a practical way, as I think it a good one' (J. O. Mayes, Cuba). 'The idea is one I have held for years, and I am glad to see there is hope of the unity of the English-speaking nations at last making an attempt to render wars an impossibility.' (Miss M.R. Ingham, Bournemouth, England.)

In the third issue of *The Landmark*, a concerned lady from Wales asked, 'Are women eligible for membership?' and was assured by the editor (Wrench) that, 'Women are of course eligible for membership in E.S.U.' With grave courtesy the editor reproduced a letter from 'a scholar, aged 16 years', who 'would like to get in touch with an American boy of about the same age; especially one interested in chemistry or wireless telegraphy'. A correspondent from New South Wales was adamant in declaring, 'I wish the British and American peoples would realise that they are indeed the lost ten tribes of Israel, and are now fulfilling the high duties ordained for them of old time.' Diplomatic as ever, Wrench made no comment.

As previously noted, the amalgamation with the Atlantic Union was announced in the second issue of *The Landmark*. Subsequently a Mr John C. Shaffer, of Chicago, wrote to express his warm approval:

> I am pleased to learn that the English-Speaking Union and the Atlantic Union have been consolidated into one society or organisation and am grateful to you for having admitted me into this society. I trust that through this organisation there may be a closer and warmer friendship between the United States and Great Britain. I shall be pleased to do anything I can to help along in this matter.

Wrench pointed out that the Atlantic Union was the oldest of all the Anglo-American Societies in existence and that it 'was the pioneer of hospitality to the English-speaking visitors'. He further noted:

> The amalgamation of the two bodies involves the following points of interest:
>
> 1. The old and euphonious title of Atlantic Union will be used on the literature.
> 2. Life members of the Atlantic Union will become life members of the English-Speaking Union, receiving the magazine for one year without charge.
> 3. It is not proposed to abandon the methods of the Atlantic Union, which have made it so widely known and appreciated, but to supplement them with others more suited to the lean and strenuous years ahead.

Wrench could not have been more generous to the members of the Atlantic Union, who included Sir Arthur Conan Doyle, creator of Sherlock Holmes. He paid fulsome tribute to the good work they had done, while recording that 'The proceedings having been personal and private, no attempt has ever been made to gain publicity or attract a large number of members.' It thus appears that membership recruitment was the Achilles heel of the Atlantic Union. Wrench, of course, had a proven track record in both membership recruitment and business promotion; it is likely that these were the methods 'more suited to the lean and strenuous years ahead'. For instance, the minutes of the ESU Executive Committee of 29 August 1918 contained the resolution that '6,000 letters be sent out to American residents in the British isles' – a targeted mailshot which would do credit to any contemporary marketing campaign.

Certainly the advertising content of these early *Landmarks* demonstrate Wrench's flair for promotion. In Phineus Barnum's celebrated dictum, 'Without promotion, something dreadful happens – nothing.' Selfridges, Ingersoll and Dr Scholl must have been prime accounts, while the National Institute for the Blind and Dr Barnardo's Homes demonstrate what we would now term 'social conscience'. Did Wrench himself do the (highly competent) copywriting? One strongly suspects so. There is an intriguing and very well written early advert in *The Landmark* – perhaps an attempt at delegation – that states 'Copy-writers Wanted (Either Sex)'. How typical of Wrench, a man so far ahead of his era, to make the position open to men and women, and both full-time or part-time – most unusual for 1919.

The early *Landmarks* and the minutes of the Central Committee are complementary in illustrating the progress of the ESU over its first decade. Early on, a debit balance was noted for the *Landmark* account due to 'decrease in revenue from advertisements and increase in cost of production'. We may not easily think of Wrench as spending his time selling advertising space; but that is almost certainly what he did. The most noble of projects require 'spadework'. Wrench, like all achievers, was not above doing whatever was needed, however unglamorous.

The Atlantic Union amalgamation had been a notable success; an approach to the 'Anglo-American Society' proved less so. 'The Chairman [of the ESU] reported that a letter had been received from the Secretary, saying that, in his opinion, no useful purpose could be served by the combination of the two bodies.' A tart reply. Notwithstanding this rebuff, the greatest attribute of marketing was promptly invoked: persistence. 'It was resolved to keep in the closest touch with the active members of this Society.'

A reader of *The Landmark* had asked, 'Are women eligible for membership?' Soon it was proposed by the Central Committee 'that ladies be elected as Vice-Presidents'. It is highly likely that Lady des Voeux, Wrench's cousin, later his wife, networked skilfully. Of the first tranche of possible Vice-Presidents, there was the Duchess of Atholl, Lady Astor, Lady Clarendon and Lady des Voeux. It should be remembered that at this time women (and by no means all women) had just been granted the vote. The shortage of manpower due to the First World War had given women a long-overdue chance to demonstrate their abilities – and women's voting rights had only been achieved via considerable sacrifice. The swift co-option of ladies into the ESU showed how progressive an organisation it was. 'We would like to assure our friends of the fair sex that as far as the E-S.U. is concerned they possess equal rights ...'

Sheer pragmatism suggested that contributors of significant time and money to the ESU would probably be people of means. The bevy of titled ladies implies no snobbery. Snobbery simply had no part in Wrench's makeup. And, for all his insistence that the ESU should be the antithesis of a 'one-man-band', his is the invisible hand constantly directing it. With characteristic mildness and good humour, he wrote 'We seem to run rather freely to peeresses, but after all, it has so far pleased Providence to "leave us still our old nobility"; the VP chamber is, of course, the Upper House of the union.'

The Landmark continued to be a financial burden. It was made clear to the Committee that its financial success

> depended upon its circulation (in other words membership) being large enough to attract advertisers to it as a business proposition. The Chairman drew attention to the steady increase in advertising revenue since January last, and asked every member of the Committee to take a supply of circulars and enrol their friends.

A characteristically blunt approach to membership recruitment! Conversely a resolution was passed

> that all members [of the Central Committee] who have not made 50% of attendances during any one year (unless leave of absence has been asked and granted by resolution recorded in the minutes) be by the executive automatically struck off the list.

Active members – not dead wood – were wanted in the ESU.

Was there dissension – both on the Central Committee and elsewhere in the ESU? Almost certainly. Earlier Wrench had asked himself, 'How was it possible for there to be squabbling among workers for the cause of unity?' Ironically, organisations dedicated to causes of unity probably involve the most squabbling. Commercial organisations tend to have a relatively simple *raison d'être*, although typically there will be an invisible 'iron curtain' running down the corridor between production and sales. However, with organisations dedicated to the greater good, there are perennial questions, the most fundamental of which is *whose* greater good? For instance, regarding 'definition of the term "English-Speaking" as regards eligibility for membership', the Central Committee noted that 'Dr Muirhead's suggestion that "English-Speaking" should mean British subjects whose mother tongue was English was received, but it was decided not to draw up any definite rules, and to decide each case on its merits.' A very wise decision, for which Wrench may have had to lobby strenuously. After all, the citizens of the United States of America (joining the ESU in 1920) were hardly 'British subjects'. The whole point of the ESU was to bridge cultural chasms. The tolerance behind deciding 'each case on its merits' almost certainly paved the way for Bermuda, Australia, New Zealand and Canada to become early joiners of the ESU.

A decision to make one of the ESU headquarters rooms non-smoking (for the ladies?) was reversed at the next Committee meeting just five days later, while at that same meeting 'the suggestion from the Chair that women should sit on the Central Committee was not adopted'. One has a sense of Wrench wrestling with reactionary forces. Shortly afterwards, a series of rules for members' club rooms were approved. Reading between the lines, one visualises Wrench struggling to prevent the premises being turned over to (male) high jinks.

On the plus side, some good news was received:

> The Editor reported that the Anglo-American Oil Company [one of the advertisers in *The Landmark*] had taken six pages at £15 net each for a special article in the May issue and 8,000 copies of the magazine for distribution. It was decided to try to secure similar contracts with other firms.

Elsewhere there is a tantalising reference to a visit by Wrench to Paris regarding the proposed opening of a French branch. Sadly this would have to wait for another sixty years. And a suggestion by a Mr Giller that the ESU open in Belgium received enthusiastic approval by Wrench. Interestingly, the multilingual and multicultural city of Brussels would pave the way for the ESU in Europe in the 1970s. But these odd snippets back in the early 1920s, just a few years after the birth of the ESU, show that Wrench was no mere 'Anglo-American' as is often claimed.

Reading the minutes of the meetings of the Executive Committee in the 1920s, the ESU's first decade, one is struck by a sense of businesslike order, of discipline, of rigour. Wrench was with the ESU for the long haul. There must have been many times when his entrepreneur's spirit chafed against bureaucratic inertia. But he had determined that the ESU should be more than a one-man-band and he stuck doggedly to his promise. The mountaineering classic *Annapurna*, the account of the first ascent of an 8,000-metre peak, tells a tale of ecstatic triumph followed by terrible suffering. It ends with the timeless aphorism: 'There are other Annapurnas in the lives of men.' As Maurice Herzog swapped the ecstasy and agony of Annapurna for many decades of bureaucratic struggle for similarly noble aims, so Evelyn Wrench, an inspired 'ideas man', adjusted to the inexorable grind of being an 'organisation man'. Long ago his mystical experiences had culminated in the realisation that his life must be devoted to the greater good. So be it. Wrench was not one to shirk his duty.

The ESU expanded to the US in 1920, to Australia and Bermuda in 1922, to Canada in 1923 and to New Zealand in 1924. Apart from Scotland in 1952, and Pakistan in 1961, these would be the only openings in new countries until 1975. Although the ESU was originally Commonwealth-based, the Belgian suggestion and the Paris initiative show how Wrench's mind was working. There must have been many times when his vision must have soared far beyond what was being achieved in practice. Yet he persevered with the necessary minutiae.

From its inception, the spirited articles in *The Landmark* pay vivid testimony to the power of the ESU to promote lively debate between people of different nations and sharply opposing views. Today's young entrants in ESU-sponsored debates might be surprised by the trenchant manner with which some of these views were expressed. For instance, the very formation of the ESU invoked this bitter letter to the editor:

> I am astonished at the stupidity with which the society is being launched ... Apparently a few American & Englishmen whose names appear in connection with similar efforts are creating the Union without any consideration of the other English Speaking nations such as Canada, Australia, the Cape etc ... the manner in which the US is placed first is perhaps only what one might expect in this present day, when Great Britain seems to be doing everything she can to flatter the great Republic.

The author of this splenetic piece was either unaware of or indifferent to an ESU-inspired memorial service for US servicemen in Westminster Abbey the previous year. Replying to the letter, Wrench was characteristically far too polite to draw this service to people's attention. Instead he commented mildly but firmly, 'If our movement has not spread readily in Canada so far, neither the New York nor London organisation can be blamed. Nothing would please us more than to have a powerful Canadian branch.'

Of course, within a decade of this letter, both Australian and Canadian ESUs had opened. And Wrench's enthusiasm for French and Belgian ESUs showed a concern for countries where English was a second, not a first language. The letter-writer's rather mean-spirited diatribe about America ignored so many factors such as: the huge importance of the United States entering the war; the ensuing *rapprochement* between the United States and Great Britain; Evelyn Wrench's lifetime ambition of drawing these two nations together; the conviction, held by so many eminent figures, that the greatest chance of world peace lay precisely in this *rapprochement* between the United States and Great Britain.

Regarding this last, vital point, it is worth quoting what three deeply concerned people said at the time:

> 'I believe that all our plans for preventing future wars must be based upon a union of thought and sentiment, and mutual help of the Anglo-Saxon peoples.' (General John J. Pershing)
>
> 'The Government recognises that largely the future welfare of the world turns upon the relations between the two countries [Britain and America].' (Andrew Bonar Law, speech to the House of Commons)
>
> 'It has always been my earnest wish that the relations between the two great English-speaking nations should be of the closest and most friendly nature, and that they should work together hand in hand for the good of civilisation and mankind'. (HM King George V)

Despite this implicit approval, Wrench was never in any doubt that 'ES cooperation must rest on mutual advantage or its foundations will prove to be of sand'. He admitted that 'during the past few months the task of those who believe in the vital necessity of promoting a warm friendship between the English-speaking peoples has not been an easy one, and we at the ESU have had our sincerity put to the test'. Indeed the ESU's sincerity was put to the test from many quarters. As *The Landmark* commented:

> There are one or two faint-hearted individuals who in our early days said that any attempt on the part of the English-speaking peoples

to get together would be resented by our French and Italian friends. This prophecy has, of course, proved a false one. It is realised across the Channel that there is nothing in the aims and objects of the E-S.U. incompatible with our friendship for all peoples.

At least the unequivocal support of many readers must have been heart-warming. 'I have got four new members and may be able to get more,' wrote Bertha Buckley of Moundsmere Manor, Basingstoke. Mr O. P. Beeman of Hook asked, 'Have you any representatives in Bermuda?' and indicated a contact. (Presumably this initiative bore fruit as Bermuda quickly 'entered the fold'.) Mrs L. Happer, of Payton House, Stratford-upon-Avon, offered her support. 'I shall be glad to keep in touch with this very excellent organisation – wherever I am. You ask me if I can help you when you establish a branch in Japan. I shall be glad to do anything I can ...' Although the Japanese opening would not occur for many years, it is heartening to know that the worldwide vision of the ESU was present at the outset.

In 'The Trials of an Editor' Wrench noted that 'The task of editing *The Landmark* is no easy one, for however careful one may be, sooner or later one is certain to run counter to the susceptibilities of some people.' Genially he invited his readers 'for a moment, to put themselves in my shoes'. Going one stage further, he asked, 'May I share with my readers the criticisms I have received so far?' And he proceeded to enumerate them. For instance, 'One writer in England informs me that there is "too much America" in our magazine ... Surely 50 per cent American and 50 per cent British material is the goal to aim at.' Elsewhere, there was 'too much' of this and 'too much' of that ... 'Finally,' Wrench admitted, 'my remarks on the question of hereditary titles have prompted two members in Great Britain to accuse me of Bolshevism!'

Interestingly, a *Landmark* article entitled 'At Home with the Bolshevists' gave an interview by Wrench's sister, Winifride, with the noted British sculptor Mrs Clare Sheridan. Predictably there were howls of protest. As it happened, such protest was redundant for Sheridan repeatedly damned herself with her artist's loftiness, her disdain for the man in the street and, worst of all, her utter heartlessness. At times the interview struck a decidedly bizarre note. For instance, Sheridan asserted that, 'One reason why I was so happy in Russia was because of the freedom.' (One would have loved to see Winifride Wrench's face at this juncture!) 'Freedom?' I queried. 'Yes,' she said enthusiastically. 'Don't you see, all an artist wants is WORK and FOOD. I had heaps of interesting work to do, and was provided with food and lodging ... I had an extraordinary sense of something absolutely new and fresh,' Mrs Sheridan trilled. 'All the old landmarks gone. The atmosphere is so new, so young, so vital. You meet no old people in the streets and no ill ones.' 'Where are they?' I ventured. 'Dead or exiled. The few that remain have to go into homes. You see, every one must work ...' Although Sheridan's pen-portraits of Lenin, Trotsky and 'Dsirjinsky' [Felix Dzerzhinsky], 'the Savonarola of the Revolution' were undoubtedly perceptive, perhaps she was unaware of Lenin's contempt of intellectuals as 'useful idiots'. Or maybe not so useful, on this occasion, as Sheridan proudly declaimed, 'My last word? Well, if there is no food for the body in Russia, there is food for the soul.'

One cannot read the Sheridan interview without shuddering. Wrench felt obliged to make an editorial reply.

> *The Landmark* is, of course, opposed to Bolshevism in any shape or form and the interview with Mrs Sheridan ... is, in our opinion, the more damaging to Bolshevism by reason of the several vital points brought out by the writer which Mrs Sheridan was unable to answer.

Sheridan's enthusiasm for Bolshevism was probably the most controversial example of the much-prized intellectual freedom espoused by the journal. Rightly, Wrench commented that, '*The Landmark* is the cornerstone on which our whole structure is erected.' At around the same time it published a letter, then an article by T. E. Lawrence with whom Wrench remained on friendly terms. *The Landmark* gave a wide variety of people a much-needed forum in which to air their beliefs and opinions. Wrench benevolently supervised the proceedings in a manner which would have done credit to any internet moderator today. His obvious impartiality and honesty must have made many converts to intellectual tolerance.

Wrench was what we might term a 'multiplier'. Multipliers (those in the influencing professions, such as teachers or journalists) are positioned to exercise powerful influences – whether for good or ill – upon large numbers of people. Frequently those whom they influence are so moved by the experience that they, in turn, influence many others. And so on. It is impossible to chart how many ripples there are and how far they travel, but multipliers can act as catalysts for major social change. In 'The Alumnus Experience' we shall hear the accounts of ESU alumni, many of them multipliers, who have effected beneficial change both within their professions and across society as a whole. Through picking likely leaders of tomorrow and giving them access to 'the alumnus experience', i.e. ESU programmes at vital junctures in their lives, the benefits to society have been massively multiplied.

Wrench's struggles with narrow-mindedness must have seemed never-ending. In a brief essay entitled 'A Few Pessimists', he wrote:

> Even in the ranks of the E-S.U there are a few pessimists who, every time that some phase of Anglo-American friendship becomes a little difficult, lose confidence in the great cause which we represent and indulge in the gloomiest forebodings as to the unnaturalness of any coming together and co-operation between the two great sections of the English-speaking world. During the past month I have received two letters, one from a gloomy American and another from a gloomy Englishman, both of whom told in almost identical terms the same woeful story. My English correspondent wrote as follows, and in the cause of Anglo-American amity I reproduce his words: 'I do not believe we shall ever turn the U.S.A. into a friendly nation – they hate us, and we despise their bombast – that is, of course, as a nation – individually they are delightful acquaintances, but not friends ...'
>
> Unfortunately I misplaced my American correspondent's letter, but it was somewhat as follows: 'Despite all the Anglo-American post-prandial orators, I do not believe the Britishers ever really like us. Englishmen have never got over the American revolution and never will. Foreign nations we are, and foreign nations we shall remain.'

In another brief essay entitled 'The Mists of Understanding', Wrench gave an admirable reply:

> I think that the best answer I can give to my two correspondents is to put them in touch with one another. If they would only come and sit in my editorial chair for a week and read the letters which reach the E-S.U. London offices from all parts of the United States and the British Commonwealth, they would, I feel sure, change their points of view. While I do not for a moment pretend that

even the majority of the two sections of the English-speaking people really understand one another and appreciate the other's sterling qualities, I do most earnestly believe that the number of individuals on both sides of the Atlantic and throughout the English-speaking world who realise the community of interests of both our peoples is an ever-increasing one. Despite the pessimists, I was never more certain than I am today that the task of making us better known to one another is destined in the course of time completely to disperse those mists of misunderstanding which have kept us apart in the past.

Re 'Anglo-American post-prandial orators', *The Landmark* gave fascinating quotations such as:

'We English and you Americans are one people, not because we speak the same language, but because our root ideas are the same.' (Joseph Chamberlain)

'We who speak American and you who speak English are conscious of a community which no differences can take from us.' (John Galsworthy)

'The penetrating vision of Cecil Rhodes foresaw that a mutual understanding between the people of the British and American Commonwealths would become a necessity for the future peace and security of the world.' (Sir G.R. Parkin, Secretary of the Rhodes Trust)

In 1921 Winston Churchill accepted the position of Chairman of the ESU. He was unequivocal in his support: 'The particular work in which you are engaged is marching hand in hand with the great destiny of our races in the world.' Dr Frank Crane amplified this argument: 'The ESU has its chief value in the fact that it is an effort to think of ourselves in larger terms. The spirit that actuates the ESU is not empire, which means control over other nations, but federation, which means an understanding with other nations.'

The 'understanding with other nations' continued apace. In 1923 the first Walter Hines Page Travelling Scholarship for teachers came into being and its recipient travelled to the United States. The following year the directors of the Chautauqua Institution offered two similar scholarships to British women. *The Landmark* referred to this as a 'great summer intellectual picnic'. Shortly afterwards, the first Walter Page Memorial Lecture was given. Wrench was determined that the memory of Dr Page would become enshrined in the ESU. Discourse with Dr

Page and Frank Doubleday had provided much-needed intellectual nourishment for his original ideas about 'the special relationship' and, of course, Dr Page's approval of Wrench's idea of forming the ESU had come at exactly the right time. Sometimes we all need that extra push to get us beyond self-doubt – and Dr Page gave it.

As the first decade – one of quiet, steady success – of the ESU drew to an end, Evelyn Wrench became increasingly preoccupied with finding new premises for this organisation which he had brought into being and nourished with such devotion and love. These new premises needed to be more than just a centre for the ESU. They also needed to become its spiritual home. After the inevitable searching and a lengthy appeal for funds, Wrench finally announced the purchase of a particular property. He promised that 'no secular building in London or in any other part of the British Commonwealth will be devoted to a more worthy purpose'. The building, in the heart of London's Mayfair, was called Dartmouth House.

3
The ESU and Dartmouth House

'Another distinguishing aspect of our identity is Dartmouth House ... a jewel and a very important source of revenue. In the very heart of the West End, we have one of its most desirable locations. But also one redolent with history. After all, Winston Churchill lived just down the road ...' (Lord Watson)

In 1066, William, Duke of Normandy, crossed the Channel with a fleet of warships to invade England. At the Battle of Hastings, he defeated King Harold Godwinson, who died, it is claimed, of an arrow piercing his eye. With the so-called Norman Conquest, rule of England changed from Anglo-Saxon to Norman. With the passing of time, two sharply-opposing cultures intermingled. It has been suggested that this intermingling of Anglo-Saxon and Norman characteristics gave rise to a distinctively British temperament, which would, many centuries later, create the greatest empire since Rome.

Evelyn Wrench, born of the last tranche of British imperialists, grew to witness a much-changed world order. Conversely, he was one of the first to realise that Britain had more subtle, and perhaps equally valuable, post-imperial gifts for the world.

No empire will long survive without established systems of control. The Romans, accomplished imperialists, understood this well. Six hundred years had elapsed between the last Roman legions departing Britain and the invasion of William of Normandy in 1066. The island had been invaded repeatedly by the inhabitants of northern Germany and southern Scandinavia. King William I of England – 'the Conqueror' – brought in a new, much more sophisticated form of government. As with the Romans, he understood the value of control systems. One of his innovations was the Domesday Book, completed twenty years after the invasion, in 1086. This systematically listed ownership of land and livestock throughout the country. Once the Domesday Book was in place, taxation became a relatively simple matter. 'Domesday' referred to the Day of Judgement. What the

Domesday Book stipulated became law. As such, its judgement was final. There was no appeal.

At the time of the Domesday Book, the land on which Dartmouth House stands lay within the Manor of Eye, held by Geoffrey de Mandeville. Shortly afterwards Geoffrey gave it to the Abbey of Westminster, where it remained until 1536, when Henry VIII confiscated it prior to the dissolution of the Abbey. In 1554 part of the Manor known as Brick Close (so called because of clay deposits) was sold to two gentlemen, one of whom, William Jennings, bequeathed it to his grandson who held it until the first Lord Berkeley acquired it in 1675. Earlier, in 1664, Lord Berkeley had bought a nearby field for his town house – Berkeley House, Piccadilly. The diarist John Evelyn described Berkeley House as 'a sweete place'. Lord Berkeley's grandson built Berkeley Square and several nearby streets, including Charles Street, which may have been named after a member of the Berkeley family. On the opposite side of the Square to Charles Street stands Hay Hill, the last cobblestone street in central London. Nearby stands another, newer, Berkeley House, a block of spacious flats. The view from the nursery window of the plane trees of Berkeley Square is one of the earliest memories of the author of this narrative.

Charles Street dates from 1675. The first recorded ratepayer of number 37 was the Dowager Duchess of Chandos, Marchioness of Carnarvon, in 1755. Her former husband, the Duke of Chandos, is remembered for his association with Handel and Pope. Subsequent owners include the Earl of Stamford and the Marquess of Bute. Residents of number 38 include Sir John Hynds Cotton and Sir Thomas and Lady Hesketh, cousin and chief source of biographical information on the poet Cowper.

In 1870 Edward Charles Baring bought number 37 Charles Street. In 1885, three years after the birth of Evelyn Wrench, Baring was ennobled as Lord Revelstoke. In 1890 he bought number 38 Charles Street in order to turn the two Georgian houses into one larger domain, to create a showcase for his collection of Louis XV furniture and art. No expense was spared to create a home of 'rococo opulence' in the Anglo-French style, so popular during the late-Victorian era.

Lord Revelstoke commissioned William Cubitt and Co. for the exterior construction work, which included the conversion of the two properties, the re-facing of the building in stone and the building of the courtyard and mews house. The Mayfair furnishing and decorating company William Turner Lord designed the interior. It has been recorded that 'The refitting of 37/38 Charles Street for one of the most conspicuous consumers of the decade was a commission of unprecedented size and importance and ... was crucial in establishing the firm's reputation as the leading interior decorators of Mayfair.'

Lord Revelstoke's London home was an amalgamation of styles, so expertly designed by William Allwright, William Turner Lord's designer, that it is often difficult to identify what is old and what is relatively new. This was not unusual for the tastes of the late Victorians: '... much panelling from decaying Parisian hotels has been shipped to England, cleaned, regilded and neatly made up for the fashionable drawing rooms of the period.'

Although at one time it was thought that the fireplaces were nineteenth-century copies, they are actually eighteenth-century originals, one of which is a Robert Adam, originally located at Derby House, Grosvenor Square.

Features especially designed for the house included the Belgian marble staircase, the exterior iron railings, probably Coalbrookdale, the marble courtyard and an unusually grand mews house, particularly stylish even for Mayfair.

The panels in the Wedgwood Room were painted by Pierre Victor Galland, a celebrated Victorian artist, who similarly adorned ceilings and panels for distinguished residences in Europe and America. On close inspection, one can discern how Galland has cleverly worked the Baring family name into the design.

Lord Revelstoke's fifth son, Maurice Baring, became a diplomat, author and friend of such luminaries as G. K. Chesterton, Hilaire Belloc and Sarah Bernhardt. In his autobiography, the delightfully-entitled *The Puppet Show of Memory*, he has bequeathed us a memoir of daily life at Dartmouth House in the late Victorian era. Stylish living at Charles Street alternated with visits to Membland, the Barings' country house in Devon, complete with its own steam launch and yacht.

In January 1875 a six-week-old baby was brought to live at his parents' house at number 48 Charles Street. The child would, one day, become Chairman of the English-Speaking Union. Subsequently he would use the English language with an eloquence unrivalled in history, in defence of world freedom. The child's name was Winston Churchill.

In November 1890 a crisis at Barings Bank brutally curtailed further expenditure. Although refurbishment had not yet been completed, all building and design work promptly ceased and the unfortunate builder had to wait until 1893 for final payment. That summer, Christie Manson and Woods held a three-day auction of the sumptuous furnishings and *objets d'art*. Although Lord Revelstoke continued to live in the property until his death from diabetes four years later, it was a sad end to his residence at Charles Street.

Lord Dartmouth (the 6th Earl of Dartmouth) was the next owner. The mother of the first Lord Dartmouth was the cousin of the founder of the Washington family in the United States. Thus there is a subtle – if extremely tenuous – connection between George Washington and Dartmouth House.

In 1900 the most significant changes to the house were made. Three drawing rooms on the first floor were converted to two larger rooms, which are now known as the Long Drawing Room and the Small Drawing Room. These rooms have fine ornate ceilings incorporating the crest of the Dartmouth family and the date. At this time, a rather avant-garde electric lift was installed. Perhaps the final touch to the new tenure was the engraving of Lord Dartmouth's name over the front door.

Number 37 Charles Street remained the Dartmouth family home until the outbreak of the First World War in 1914. Under the supervision of Lady Lytton, the house was used by the Red Cross as a military hospital. Fireplaces and wall coverings were sealed up for protection. In 1918 the house was sold. Subsequently the Hon. Mrs Robert Lindsay occupied it from 1923 to 1926.

By the summer of 1925 the existing Members' Rooms of the ESU had clearly become inadequate. The Central Committee decided to take a bold step and invite the support of British members in an effort to purchase a distinctive residence which would become the permanent home of the English-Speaking Union. Over the following six months, various properties were considered, including several houses in St James's Square. Finally, no doubt after much heart-searching, number 37 Charles Street – or Dartmouth House as it became known - won out. It was an inspired choice. Dartmouth House is perfectly situated, in the very heart of the capital. The area, although eminently prestigious, has nothing gaudy about it; rather it is the epitome of discreet charm. And it is embassy territory – highly appropriate for an organisation which would, one day, span the world.

The purchase of the 83-roomed Dartmouth House was completed on Midsummer Day 1926. As Evelyn Wrench proudly asserted, 'No secular building in London, or in any other part of the British Commonwealth will be devoted to a more worthy purpose.' Mr St Loe Strachey, editor of *The Spectator* and ESU Vice-Chairman, recommended his son-in-law, Clough Williams-Ellis (of Portmeirion fame), as a young architect capable of transforming this rather neglected and outmoded Victorian house into the busy Headquarters of the English-Speaking Union. In the event, few major structural alterations were needed. A ground-floor panelled room was turned into the Walter Hines Page Memorial Library and restaurants, bedrooms and sitting rooms were created. On New Year's Day 1927 the premises were made available to ESU members. The formal opening of Dartmouth House was made in 1927 by the Prime Minister, Stanley Baldwin, on George Washington's birthday, 22 February, in the presence of the American Ambassador and a most distinguished gathering. Lord Balfour and Lord Reading made speeches. In Evelyn Wrench's words, 'Dartmouth House symbolises our aims, a freehold building belonging to our members, dedicated to the difficult task of promoting fellowship among the people who speak English.' On a more practical note, Clough Williams-Ellis's autobiography mentions him being fearful for the safety of those attending the opening of the building. When he realised that the speeches were to be made on the marble staircase, he doubted that it would carry so many people. Afraid that it would collapse, along with so many distinguished luminaries, including the Prime Minister and the American Ambassador, he attempted to redistribute them and was much relieved when the ceremony was over. (Present-day visitors please note: the staircase is entirely safe!)

From the onset, the accommodation at Dartmouth House was of a very high standard indeed. The marbled Staircase Hall and the Main Staircase were described as 'perhaps the most striking features of the house'. The Dining Rooms (currently the Wedgwood Room and the Revelstoke Room), on the right of the Reception Hall, could accommodate up to seventy diners. The marbled, eight-foot-wide staircase, with its steel balustrade, adorned with a design incorporating the Revelstoke monogram, led to the main public rooms on the first floor; the Drawing Room (now known as the Long Drawing Room), the Ballroom, the Ladies' Private Drawing Room (now the Small Drawing Room), the Tea Room and the Reading and Writing Room.

The Drawing Room, it was written, 'has been furnished to look like the main room of a comfortable old English house ... the walls will remain covered by the original green silk.' Next to the Drawing Room was the Ballroom, panelled in walnut and decorated with gilt, with an immaculately polished oak floor. This was used as the Tea Room and General Lounge. Beyond lay the Reading and Writing Room. (Later this became known as the Nell Gwynne Room, from its wood carving attributed to Grinling Gibbons, arguably the greatest wood carver in history, and reputedly purchased by Nell Gwynne, mistress of King Charles II, for one of her homes.) This 'is the lightest room in the house and was formerly the Music Room. It overlooks the courtyard and is very lofty, with a remarkable ceiling and an enormous open fireplace faced with blue-green Persian tiles ... the whole house is heated by central heating and ... to maintain the traditional cheerfulness of the English hearth, wood will be burned in the main reception rooms, and with logs piled high, the Writing Room should be one of the most sought-after rooms in the building.' The Ladies Private Drawing Room was characterised by a beautiful striped green silk tapestry.

Each of the 38 members' bedrooms had its distinctive character. The Queen Elizabeth Room housed an oak chest from the Tudor period. The John Bunyan Room held an original Bible box. Queen Mary donated an overmantel for one of the rooms, which was subsequently named after her. Each bedroom had its own writing table and telephone, the latter cutting-edge technology indeed for 1927, albeit increasingly necessary for those conducting extensive business and political careers. The modern and the historic were carefully entwined. Apropos of the latter, a congratulatory letter arrived from the Editor of *The Forum* in New York: 'I understand that Dartmouth House is in the district of haunted houses ...' As it happens, there have been several sightings of a ghostly lady on the staircase.

In short, no effort was spared to make a visit to Dartmouth House both enjoyable and memorable. The original estimate of £6,670 to kit out the house with everything from kitchen utensils to livery for the doorman was found to be woefully inadequate. Donations were sought to raise the extra funding and members nobly responded from all around the world. The result was a superb tribute to their generosity. For instance, adjoining the Reception Hall was the Bureau, which housed the activities of Travel, Shopping and General Service Bureaux respectively. Here bedrooms could be booked and tickets bought for

Volume I. Number 1.

The LANDMARK

The Monthly Magazine of The English-Speaking Union

"*This union bids fair to rank for ever amongst the great historic landmarks in the moral and political history of mankind.*"—THE TIMES, June 28, 1917.

January, 1919

FEATURES THIS MONTH

The Future of the World By THE RT. HON. A. J. BALFOUR

America at War and After By LORD SYDENHAM OF COMBE

Materialism and Idealism in America By GEORGE SANTAYANA, PH.D., LITT.D.

War Savings in England By SIR ROBERT KINDERSLEY, K.B.E.

The Returned Soldier in Public Affairs By F. P. GLASS, ESQ. (Editor of the *Birmingham* (Alabama) *News*).

PUBLISHED FOR THE LANDMARK PUBLISHING COMPANY BY
CAHILL & CO., LTD., 43 NEW OXFORD STREET,
LONDON, W.C.

PRICE ONE SHILLING NET IN GREAT BRITAIN. TWENTY-FIVE CENTS IN THE UNITED STATES.

The first issue of *The Landmark*, journal of the ESU

Evelyn Wrench, founder of the English-Speaking Union

The portrait of Dr Walter Hines Page in the Revelstoke Room at Dartmouth House

Blitz children writing letters to their American benefactors

An ESU-sponsored wartime event. Phyllis Biscoe on extreme right.

sightseeing trips and functions. Travel plans were prepared by the Manager, with special attention to the then novel mode of 'motor car travel'. It was noted that 'Steamship and railway tickets, theatre and concert tickets can also be secured.' It was also recorded that 'By arrangement with the Postmaster-General, a private posting box has been installed in the Entrance Hall and members' letters will be collected at stated times.'

Ever mindful of hospitality towards American visitors, 'an English butler has been engaged who was, for several years, in one of the best clubs in New York and who has therefore practical knowledge of the requirements of both British and American members'. The Page Memorial Library commemorated an American connection of integral importance for the ESU. To quote an early ESU publicity leaflet:

> The honour of establishing a library in memory of the late Walter Hines Page was entrusted to the English-Speaking Union by the Trustees of the Page Memorial Committee, and the Page Memorial Library may now be considered to be, in a modest way, a representative collection of British-American literature.
>
> On one wall hangs Mr P. A. de Laszlo's replica of his original portrait of Dr Page in his robes of an Hon. DCI while, in a special place of honour, stands a heavy cut-glass inkstand, the property of the Ambassador himself, and graciously given to the ESU by his widow.

1932 brought official recognition of the Herculean efforts of Evelyn Wrench in forming the ESU and helping to guide it through its first turbulent decade. He became Sir Evelyn Wrench. Few knighthoods can have been more richly deserved. The Queen visited Dartmouth House. A year later The Prince of Wales accepted the office of President – establishing a royal connection which has continued to the present day. His percipient observation remains as true now as when it was first made: '... It is especially important that the English-speaking peoples should maintain a sympathetic understanding of each other's problems and should not allow the difficulties of the moment to obscure a fundamental unity of interest.'

Dartmouth House hosted a reception for delegates to the world economic conference from the British Dominions and the United States. This, together with the royal visit, underlined the wisdom of making the move to Charles Street. Dartmouth House had proved pivotal to the acceptance of the ESU as an international organisation of the highest order. In August 1936 Wrench proposed an extension. The then significant sum of £20,000 was required in donations. Shortly afterwards, in February 1937, the ESU acquired adjoining premises in 34–36 Charles Street at a cost of £21,000. The ESU was expanding and, with the onset of the Second World War shortly afterwards, every scrap of space would be put to good use.

After the war, in the 1960s, the ESU bought the freehold of three previously rented houses adjoining Dartmouth House with the intention of rebuilding them as modern club premises. 1972 saw the signing of a 99-year lease for 34–36 Charles Street to Grand Metropolitan Hotels. ESU club members would be compensated for the loss of their premises by receiving discounted hotel rates. Grand Metropolitan paid a premium of £100,000 (then a very considerable sum), while the ESU maintained the freehold of the lease as a hedge against future inflation. In addition to the £100,000, the ESU also received a tourism grant of £80,000 for having leased the premises as a hotel instead of a club. The first down-payment of rent was earmarked for the, by then, sadly needed redecoration of Dartmouth House.

The 1970s was an economically troubled time, with rampant inflation. The ESU suffered, as did the entire country. Financial difficulties prompted a search for other, less expensive alternatives. Through the efforts of a number of devoted people, it was possible to remain at Charles Street. We are in their debt.

Exactly the same issue surfaced in the early 1980s and early 2000s, two more periods of economic woe. Once again alternatives were sought; once again the 'friends of Dartmouth House' fought for its survival.

Houses have their distinctive characters. For so many people who have given decades of their lives to furthering the cause of international friendship, Dartmouth House is the soul of the ESU. Any other location is, quite simply, unthinkable. Certainly, over the intervening decades, there have been many prestigious gatherings at Dartmouth House. It has proved a tremendous asset. But Dartmouth House is not an embassy owned by a country. It is not a Head Office owned by a bank or an advertising agency. It is the meeting place and the working office of a membership organisation. This means that, irrespective of the eminence of those, such as prime ministers and ambassadors, who have graced its elegant rooms, its finances have to be earned. The present-day arrangement with Leith's restaurateurs means that people can dine splendidly in the very heart of Mayfair at surprisingly modest prices. The author of this book can testify that lunch at Dartmouth House is to be savoured.

'We must make Dartmouth House as beautiful as we can,' said Lady Eccles with courage and resolution even amid the financial turmoil of the 1970s. The then Director-General, Hugh Jones, paid her the graceful compliment that 'Dartmouth House was certainly a palace we could be proud of thanks to her efforts'. The spirit of reviving its grandeur and style was taken up once more in the early 2000s by the eminent architect Graham Mitchell. Visit Dartmouth House today and you cannot fail to recognise that you are in the presence of a labour of love made possible by the efforts of many. Lord Revelstoke, the tragic inspirer of Dartmouth House, would warmly approve; and so too would Sir Evelyn Wrench.

4
The ESU At War

'... we saw the flags of all the nations floodlit at Westminster, the Union Jack on the Abbey floating like liquid fire ... There, in that great crowd, where we were all one – there, that moment was perfect, and I could have died of happiness! It had all been so worthwhile.' (Pamela Blaxlard)

We have seen how, in the aftermath of the First World War, Evelyn Wrench had met the young and deeply charismatic T. E. Lawrence. Wrench had published Lawrence in *The Landmark* and helped him try to get a fairer hearing for the cause of the Arab peoples. Subsequently Lawrence turned his back on society for the obscurity of lowly enlisted service in the RAF. However the two men, so very different in temperament, remained firm friends.

On 13 May 1935 Wrench was due to visit Lawrence at his cottage, Clouds Hill, near Wareham in Dorset, when he received word that his ailing mother's medical condition had worsened. Understandably he hastened to her bedside; the visit to Lawrence failed to take place. Instead of meeting Wrench, Lawrence rode out on his powerful motorbike. Swerving to avoid two boys on their bicycles, he lost control and was thrown over the handlebars. He died a few days later.

'If only ...' must be the saddest words in the English language. For poor Wrench: '... if only I had carried out my original intention, in all probability Lawrence and I would have spent some hours talking on that morning, and he would certainly have not gone for that tragic ride at the hour he did!'

The Prince of Wales had become the President of the ESU. As King Edward VIII, he declared his intention to grant his patronage to the ESU of the British Empire. However, on 11 December 1936 he abdicated. The following year, his successor, King George VI, granted his patronage to the ESU.

Taking the opportunity to comment on Sir Evelyn Wrench, the Archbishop of Canterbury noted, 'and let me add, as is fitting in a founder of the ESU, he knows how to speak and write good English.'

The compliment was well deserved. The conduct and minutes of hundreds of committee meetings, the torrent of letters to friends and supporters and the inspired editorship of *The Landmark* bear witness to Sir Evelyn's command of both the spoken and the written word. Although we inhabit a very different world, the need for skilled communication has never been greater. Should any young student in an ESU-administered programme ever feel the need for an exemplar, then they need look no further than Sir Evelyn Wrench.

On a personal note, in 1937 Sir Evelyn became engaged to his cousin, Lady des Voeux, who had been a strong supporter of the ESU from its earliest days. Subsequently the married couple's honeymoon to the US became extended to a world trip lasting several years. We must not begrudge Sir Evelyn his happiness or the welcome respite of an extended rest from the rigours of running the ESU. Sir Frederick Whyte was appointed to the newly created post of Director-General of the ESU of the British Empire. And, even on holiday, Wrench was still putting his alert, inventive mind to good use on behalf of the ESU. For instance, in the US he discovered that *The Landmark*, the title of the ESU's magazine, was not well understood and 'to new readers at least, conveyed little of what we were trying to do'. The title was thereby changed to *English Speaking World*. Interestingly, this was not so very different from the *Monthly Magazine of the English-Speaking Union*, which had first been proposed all those years before, back in 1919.

By the late 1930s, the rise of Nazi Germany posed a clear danger to the political stability of Europe. By contrast, the US was isolationist. Only twenty years had passed since young American boys had gone to war and not returned; memories were still raw. Although perturbed by isolationism, Wrench had a Victorian's stoicism:

> ... gladly accept cooperation when you get it, but for heaven's sake, don't put yourself in the position of going, as it were, hat in hand to America and wanting America to help you. That is the worst thing this country could do.

He then added:

> If however, the forces of isolationism in the US are so strong as to prevent cooperation between our two countries then I think that the British government, under Mr Neville Chamberlain, will probably do a deal with the dictatorships to preserve the peace of Europe.

He was right. September 1938 saw the historic Munich agreement, Chamberlain's famous 'peace in our time'. The editorial of the newly renamed *English Speaking World* commented that 'it seemed as if only a miracle could save us, but the miracle took place and we are at peace.' But the miracle was little more than political chimera; it satisfied no one. And a former Chairman of the ESU, Winston Churchill, was correct to snap, 'The idea that safety can be purchased by throwing a small state to the wolves is a fatal delusion.'

It was a desperately painful time. With characteristic intellectual honesty, Sir Evelyn questioned, 'Are the principles on which the ESU was based twenty-one years ago, when we optimistically hoped that a saner world order would emerge after the war, still sound?' Or, if those principles were not sound, 'should the basis of the movement be changed fundamentally?'

There was no easy answer. On 3 September 1939, after the unprovoked invasion of Poland, war was declared between Great Britain and Germany. At one stroke, over twenty years of peace was undone. The horror began, all over again.

At the outbreak of war, many ESU members left London for the relative safety of the country. Dartmouth House stood virtually empty. Subscription revenues dropped. The number of staff had to be reduced drastically. From abroad, Sir Evelyn promptly wrote a letter which appeared in the September issue of *English Speaking World*, urging members to continue using Dartmouth House. 'The English-Speaking Union was born twenty-one years ago during the Great War and it has an even greater function to play in the present crisis.' Rightly, Sir Evelyn railed against defeatism. However, it had to be admitted that 'It is a painful thought to many of its supporters on both sides of the Atlantic that their faith in an ultimate common purpose is not more widely held.'

Dartmouth House remained open. Operations continued, albeit on a reduced scale. The basement was converted into an air-raid shelter. Windows overlooking Charles Street were boarded up, shuttered and sandbagged. In case of chemical attack, gas-proof curtains were put up. Struggling to put a brave face on things, *English Speaking World* printed an article on 'Fashion in the Shelters'.

The ESU's Education Department was determined that the scholarship programmes to the United States should continue. In September 1939, only days after war had been declared, twenty young scholars set sail for New York on the SS *Mauretania*. In camouflage-grey and with two large guns attached, the *Mauretania* was prepared for enemy attack. Thankfully the trip was without mishap. Much to their parents' relief, all the boys arrived safely in New York and were despatched to their new schools. Although a number of scholarships for female teachers were taken up during 1939–40, due to the war effort no male teaching scholarships were filled. In the United States the exchange of American teachers and scholars ceased for the duration of the war.

In the First World War Evelyn Wrench's innovations had greatly helped. Now, in a letter to *The Times*, he suggested that the ESU assume responsibility for overseas evacuation of children to America. Although this idea was not adopted, the role of the ESU changed in another way. As the first winter of the war approached, supplies of money and clothing began to arrive at Dartmouth House from the United States. Some of these donations were earmarked for particular cases, which included crews of fifty ex-American destroyers, refugees, British servicemen and evacuees. Non-earmarked items were distributed by the ESU to those in need. Anticipating the bombing of London in the first months of the war, large numbers of children were evacuated to the country. From America came clothing, toys and sweets to assuage the anguish of their separation from parents, brothers, sisters and homes. With the characteristic good-heartedness and generosity of Americans, the ESU received offers of accommodation of British children with US families. Many of these offers were gratefully accepted until the evacuation of children to the US stopped in November 1940. A ship named the *City of Benares* sank and eighty-five children died.

The Battle of Britain began in July 1940. It took its name from a speech given by a former Chairman of the ESU, Prime Minister Winston Churchill, in the House of Commons. 'The Battle of France is over. I expect the Battle of Britain is about to begin ...' He was right; it did. The German Air Force, the Luftwaffe, mounted an all-out effort to gain air superiority over the Royal Air Force, especially Fighter Command. Such superiority could have been used as a prelude to Hitler's Operation Sealion, an amphibious and airborne invasion of Britain. Heavily outnumbered, the RAF determinedly fought back. In the fields of Southern England, workers, raising food for the nation, could see their fate being determined, day after day, in the skies above their heads. There were acts of desperate courage on both sides. Churchill, as so often, had the last memorable word: 'Never in the field of human conflict was so much owed by so many to so few.' Thenceforth those young men who fought in the Battle of Britain would be known as 'The Few'.

By October it was clear that the Nazis had lost the Battle of Britain. Air superiority was denied them. Nevertheless the Blitz – the sustained bombing of London and other British cities by the Luftwaffe – had begun the month before. The worst of it lasted until May 1941. It was both an attempt to bring Britain to logistical deadlock and an attempt to break the British spirit. It is said that, even for trained, battle-hardened soldiers, the experience of being under mortar bombardment rapidly becomes psychologically shattering. In the Blitz, the entire civilian populations of London and other cities were under similar bombardment. At any time, death could fall from the skies.

'The English-Speaking Union ... has an even greater function to play in the present crisis.' Sir Evelyn's words were prescient. From late 1939 to 1943 a 'transatlantic bridge' was created between the ESU North American headquarters and Dartmouth House. The American-inspired flow of goods and money to a beleaguered London gave immense practical support. The film star Cary Grant and the much-loved singer Gracie Fields donated the equivalent of more than £500,000 in today's money. Naturally most donations were much smaller and came from a legion of individual ESU members. All of them were gratefully welcomed.

It must be remembered that, at this time, the US was not yet at war. Strict neutrality laws governed what might and what might not be sent across the Atlantic. However it seems that sending items as 'gifts' provided a legal loophole. Before long, both ambulances and canteens arrived as 'gifts' – and even small arms for the Home Guard.

Of course that is what they were and personalised as such, with letters to the recipients, many of whom wrote back to express their gratitude. If there was no sender's name or address attached, people would write to Phyllis Biscoe or Alice Gardiner, the relevant department heads at Dartmouth House. This excerpt, from one of thousands of letters received by the ESU, came from 'Ron' and is reproduced exactly as he wrote it.

> Dear American people: I am so happy to have this great pleasure of writing. Thank you ever so much for the nice new clothes and I

> am so happy as can be. I think I should thank you American people who have helped to get my clothes. For my mother has trouble to get them in England. I don't know how to thank you all ... every time I put these clothes on in the morning, it always makes me think of that song called America I Love You.
>
> All my love and good wishes for America, Russia and England to have a big smack at Hitler and end this terrible war.
>
> Goodbye, your loving British friend
>
> Ron

One of the letters was especially poignant. It came from a young boy who had experienced the upheaval of being evacuated from London. An ESU member in the United States had sent him socks, gloves and a hat. The little fellow wrote back:

> Thank you for the socks and gloves and hat. We have had a lot of snow and they kept me warm. My dad is in the Royal Air Force and a bomb fell on our house but Mummy found some knives and forks left. I like the garden here and the rabbits. We didn't have them in London. I am seven.

On 5 February 1941 HM Queen Elizabeth visited Dartmouth House. She was shown this letter and was understandably moved. As Sir Evelyn was in the United States, the Queen was received by the Deputy Chairman of the ESU, Dame Edith Lyttelton. The same day, the BBC issued a radio broadcast. A Pathé News film was also made. Decades later this newsreel was discovered in the cellar of nearby Clarges Mews. In 1995, some fifty-four years after it had been made, it was shown at an ESU-inspired ceremony at the US embassy. The film is in black and white and, by modern standards, is stylised. Nevertheless the famous warmth of the Queen's personality shines through as she examined dozens of items of clothing and small gifts which had come from across the Atlantic. She added her own gratitude to our 'ever-generous American brothers and sisters'.

Although one can tentatively attempt to quantify the practical support from America to Britain via Dartmouth House, one cannot begin to quantify the moral support. The first years of the war were a bleak, terrible time, when defeat followed defeat and it seemed impossible that democracy and civilisation would prevail in Europe. For

Americans to give such visible evidence of their friendship made a huge emotional impact. Their generosity must never be forgotten.

At the US Embassy ceremony in the summer of 1995, the American Ambassador, His Excellency William J. Crowe Jr, presented the following letter to five recipients of this wartime generosity:

> This evening we remember with pride the great joint venture of the English-speaking people of the United States and the United Kingdom in bringing freedom to Europe and peace to the world 50 years ago. You will have your own special memories of that time and of the generosity of American members of the ESU. We are delighted that you are able to join us at this commemorative event on this day at the United States Embassy in London – an event symbolising the continuing friendship and alliance of our peoples, with all its promise for future years.

All those years ago, back in 1941, a Mrs Abernathy of Seattle had managed to send seven pairs of shoes and socks for English children. She added a note which said simply, 'God bless the little feet that wear these shoes.' Some of these shoes and socks had been worn by people present at the 1995 ceremony. They told the assembled audience what the generosity of unknown comrades across the Atlantic had meant to them during those dreadful years. Mrs Abernathy may be long-gone but her spirit lives on.

In 1941 alone, over £14,000 (approximately £500,000 in today's money) was donated. At Dartmouth House, the Common Interests Committee, of which Phyllis Biscoe was the Secretary, opened an emergency extension to cope with the incoming flow of gifts. However it soon became obvious that a new department would need to be created to deal with the rapidly increasing challenge of the war relief effort. Consequently an American member, Mrs Alice Gardiner, became Director of the appropriately entitled War Relief Department. Based in the garages and basements of Clarges Mews, at the height of its activity the War Relief Department had over fifteen full-time volunteers.

Working in tandem with the British War Relief Society, Dartmouth House became the hub of a daunting logistical exercise run with military precision. From the US, from Canada and from New Zealand, crates of medical equipment, blankets, clothes and toys arrived in the workrooms where they were unpacked, sorted and shelved as appropriate. Emergency calls for aid came in from all across the country;

crates of supplies were promptly despatched. With the fierce intensity of bombing in the Blitz, many of the most disadvantaged people came from London itself. These poor people, some of whom had lost close family members as well as all their possessions, found their way to Dartmouth House. Many must have been in acute distress. The ESU staff and volunteers did their absolute best, under what must often have been tragic circumstances. Nothing was wasted. Even the wood of the crates went to make shelving for the workrooms. When there was enough shelving, it was used by members of the London Fire Brigade to make toys for children who otherwise would have none.

As previously mentioned, some of the 'gifts' were sizeable: desperately needed ambulances, snackbars, blitztrailers and mobile canteens arrived from the US. The ESU gave these vehicles to the WVS, to the Red Cross and to badly blitzed areas such as Deptford and the cities of Bristol and Southampton. Gracie Fields gave all of the proceeds of her American and Canadian tours to the war effort. Some of this income was used to establish the Bristol Mothers and Babies Home in the quiet and relatively safe environs of Monmouthshire.

The ESU branches were also highly active. With the straitened financial position of Dartmouth House at the beginning of the war, they had struggled for survival. But they too changed their role to one of aid work. A particular priority was the distribution of clothing in local areas. Individual branches also dedicated themselves to particular causes according to local need. For instance, the Sussex and Kent Branch set up a Christmas fund for local anti-aircraft units.

During the Blitz, bombs fell around Dartmouth House. One day a time bomb landed but was made safe. Another day an incendiary bomb came through the roof of the Advertising Department office, setting fire to the floor. Amazingly no one was killed or even injured. The fire was put out and work quickly continued. Dartmouth House seems to have led a relatively charmed life, as many nearby houses were badly hit, particularly in Curzon Street and Shepherd Market. Amid the tragedy, there was the occasional tragic-comic episode such as the day when a neighbouring house in Charles Street was badly bombed and the drunken butler was heroically saved by the Dartmouth House porter.

By May 1941 it was obvious that – as with the Battle of Britain – the Blitz had also failed. Londoners were unbowed. Logistically the country had not ground to a standstill. With difficulty, it still functioned.

The war went on. Although British cities would continue to be bombed, the fierce intensity of the Blitz slowly abated.

On 7 December 1941 the Japanese attacked Pearl Harbor and the United States entered the war. The role of the ESU began to change once again, this time from one of aid distribution to that of providing hospitality for American forces in London. With the decreased level of bombing there was less need of immediate aid and the government took over despatch for necessary war relief. Donations from the ESU were handled by the British War Relief Society from their central warehouse, run by the Dudley House Allocation Committee. With circumstances becoming less desperate, centralisation of war relief was a sensible move which maximised the distribution efficiency of rail and shipping networks. Alice Gardiner, the Director of the War Relief Department, had done sterling work, not least in keeping the US ESU branches informed of the department's work in her weekly letters. Soon it was possible for her to return to the US. Finally, in 1943, the War Relief Committee was disbanded. Among its last activities was the presentation of a cheque from a Gracie Fields concert tour in America for the upkeep of the Convalescents Home for Boys at Charlton House. HM Queen Mary was kind enough to make a formal acceptance of this gift on behalf of the Invalid Children's Association.

From the onset of war, Dartmouth House had operated an open-door policy towards foreign servicemen and women. Some visitors came for clothing from the workrooms, while others came for free lectures and parties. In the dire days of the Blitz, keeping up morale was not merely desirable; it was essential. War routinely threw people of sharply differing backgrounds together. It was a wild, heady time. Love affairs blossomed. Why wait when there might be no tomorrow?

From 1942 onwards, the Common Interests Committee decided to concentrate on providing hospitality to Americans who were flocking into Mayfair. There were many Red Cross Clubs nearby, such as the Washington Club in Curzon Street, which was based in the former Washington Hotel. There was a PX (Services store) and an American Chapel in South Audley Street. There were two clubs for WAAFs in Charles Street. And, of course, there was the American Embassy in Grosvenor Square. The American Ambassador, John G. Winant, and his wife lived in a modest flat adjacent to the Embassy. For a time, the future American President, General Eisenhower, lived in Chesterfield Hill.

Phyllis Biscoe and her willing helpers in the Common Interests

Committee busied themselves with a variety of initiatives aimed at further increasing morale for American service personnel. Furloughs and leaves for servicemen were arranged in members' homes. There were sightseeing visits to the Houses of Parliament, the Tower of London and Eton College. Monthly dances were organised for members of the Army, Navy, Air Force, American Embassy staff, WACs and Red Cross personnel. Talks, discussions and weekly news bulletins were provided for a nearby Army base. Particularly popular were the free 'Wednesday at Seven' parties, which facilitated many a happy meeting between GIs and their future brides. These ranged from a talk by Mr Vernon Bartlett MP on 'The War Where We Stand Now' to a recital of monologues by the popular comedienne, Joyce Grenfell. It is not recorded which was more appreciated.

At Dartmouth House, the present-day Wedgwood Room, then painted pink and consequently known as the 'Pink Room', was set up as an Information Centre. Mrs Winant, the wife of the American Ambassador, opened it on 14 July 1942. *The Times* nicknamed the Information Centre 'London's Pink Room'. It was open seven days a week, from 9.30 am to 6 pm. Phyllis Biscoe ran it, with six volunteers. The success of this Information Centre inspired similar centres in the ESU branches. On 6 October 1942 Brigadier General Thiele of the US Army opened the Leicester Information Centre in offices donated by the *Leicester Evening Mail*. The wall was adorned with two large maps. Visitors were encouraged to stick a pin in their home town and to sign the visitors' book. A letter-writing service was also established. Visitors gave the addresses of loved ones back home and ESU volunteers would write to family members assuring them that sons, daughters, brothers and sisters were well. The following letter gives an indication of the emotional solace which these letters afforded:

> You do not know what peace and happiness and tears of joy your wonderful letter brought this morning. My husband and I want to thank you so much for your very welcome letter with such good news of our dear son Jack ... It is really wonderful to know that there is such a place as the ESU where our boys can get all the information and assistance they need ...
>
> (Mrs Kathleen Commnes, Brooklyn, New York)

In 1943 the Common Interests Committee extended its hospitality department into 34 Charles Street. This provided an extra club-room, complete with piano, gramophone, magazines and even a canteen. The official opening was made by Mrs Churchill, the wife of the Prime Minister, in October 1943.

It must not be thought that all this hospitality was one-way – far from it. American civilians had amply demonstrated their generosity with the plethora of gifts during the Blitz. The American servicemen and women proved no less generous. GIs were always keen to organise parties and concerts for British people, especially children, to most of whom any kind of treat was a rarity. Working in conjunction with the ESU, our American visitors and allies arranged Thanksgiving and Christmas parties for the children of Deptford. They held special Mother's Day parties on their bases, treating ESU members as surrogate mothers for the day. Doubtless this was a welcome treat for women working gruelling shifts in factories before coming home exhausted to face the inevitable burden of housework.

It must be remembered that this was a time of strict rationing; the general level of privation was well-nigh unimaginable to anyone today. When GIs were guests in members' homes, they were painfully aware that they were eating their hosts' rations – which could not be replaced. Such paltry delicacies as were served would have been agonisingly saved up over weeks and months. Of course there was a black market but most people couldn't afford it, even if they approved of it. Consequently GI visitors would always try to bring a few luxury items such as ham or eggs. After such a long spell of eating insipid egg powder, for many people just tasting a fresh egg was a real luxury.

And then, after six years of privation, of danger, and of constant uncertainty, suddenly it was all over. Pamela Blaxlard, an ESU member, kept a diary throughout the Second World War. Here is an extract, written on 9 May 1945, just after VE (Victory in Europe) Day. It marvellously conveys the tearful joy, tempered with regret for those who had paid the ultimate sacrifice.

> VE + 1 day, another holiday.
>
> I just couldn't bear it any more being in the quiet of the country while so much was happening in London. So this morning I came up to town from Crowborough, and Jack came with me. And oh, there was nowhere in the world I would rather have been but in my London, this day of victory, nor could it have been a more perfect day.

We saw Churchill, the King and Queen and Princesses on the Palace balcony, we saw the beautiful floodlighting which, after all the years of darkness, seemed to make the world a fairyland, we saw the flags of all the nations floodlit at Westminster, the Union Jack on the Abbey floating like liquid fire – perhaps the most beautiful sight of all. Everywhere we saw crowds of happy people, singing, laughing, wearing funny hats ...

We waited with the crowds outside Buckingham Palace calling, 'We want the King!', we joined in the laughter when, waiting for Churchill to come along Piccadilly this afternoon, a huge dray loaded with barrels of beer came along, and the driver, sitting high above his horses, bowed regally left and right, taking off his old cap to the delighted crowd ... And tonight, when we'd seen the King and walked past the bonfire in St James's Park to Westminster, we came by chance on the crowd listening to Churchill from the Ministry of Health balcony. Floodlights shone on him, Big Ben was brilliantly lit nearby, and all the flags so colourful against the dark sky. Then when Churchill called to us, 'Good old London!', as only he could do, he started us singing 'Rule Britannia'! There, in that great crowd, where we were all one – there, that moment was perfect, and I could have died of happiness! It had all been so worthwhile. Jack was on one side of me (it was good to have my dear cousin home from India now, even if it was his wounded leg which brought him home early), my friend Charlie, a U.S. sergeant, on the other side, and a crowd of our English and American friends from the English-Speaking Union were with us too. Earlier this evening Jack and I went to the party at the E.S.U. and he and Charlie met for the first time. (I had wondered how they would get on, my English officer cousin and my American sergeant friend, but all was well!) We stayed and danced until about 9.30, then a whole crowd of us went out to see the sights. Oh, I can't describe a millionth of all we saw, all those little incidents which occur in big crowds, always the same yet always new, and raising a laugh ... but it was all so good, so beautiful and exciting – it was our victory!

And my ever-remembered Angus, my Canadian pilot friend who played the piano so beautifully (I'll never in all my life hear the tune 'Summertime' without remembering him) and was shot down in his Spitfire over the African desert ...

It is so strange to think of Sir Evelyn Wrench's original conception of the ESU as an instrument of repayment to overseas people – particularly Americans – for their glorious traditions of hospitality. All those years of devoted service during the 1920s and 1930s were rewarded a hundredfold with the volume of gifts pouring through Dartmouth House during the Blitz. And later the generosity towards the GIs was rewarded once again.

At the service for King Edward VII in 1910, Sir Evelyn had received the answer to the greatest question that any of us will ever ask. 'I was shaken to the foundations of my being ... What was the meaning of life? Love was the key to the riddle.' The deepest expression of love is giving – without any thought of reward – simply for the joy of giving. The amazing thing is that, so very often, what is given freely is matched – or indeed exceeded – by what is given back freely. All of the giving and receiving, via Dartmouth House, the ESU branches and overseas, demonstrates this tendency.

The Second World War was a war unlike any other war in history, not just on account of its epic global scale. The stakes were the highest imaginable – the survival of civilisation itself. Defeat, however likely in those terrible early years, was quite simply unthinkable. In this battle to the death between good and evil, every act of generosity mattered. In founding the ESU, Sir Evelyn had created an extraordinary portal for international generosity and friendship. For instance, it is estimated that, in 1944 alone, more than 40,000 US service personnel were helped by the various facilities of Dartmouth House. Fifty years later, an American lady who was with the US Embassy during the Second World War, wrote a letter of gratitude and remembrance. She recorded, 'The ESU was then a major morale builder for many foreign soldiers who passed through London on their way to D-Day. I will always remember.'

Writing in 1995, Andrea Wathern, the noted ESU librarian, archivist and researcher, gave this summary of the ESU at war:

> It is difficult to estimate the number of servicemen and women and civilians that were helped by the ESU, both at Dartmouth House and the branches. Similarly it is difficult to put a final value on the many millions of items donated by the US and Dominions. The staff and volunteers of the ESU never expected to be congratulated for the work they did; there was genuine need for war relief and

hospitality and the ESU was one organisation amongst many that threw itself into the role.

It is hard to find any mention of the ESU war relief work in histories of the Second World War. Likewise it has proved difficult to find out what happened after the war to the many volunteers, such as Mrs Gardiner. We do know that Mrs Biscoe, who worked tirelessly for war relief and in hospitality, was given a CBE for the work she did during the war. Unfortunately she died in 1963 after years of struggle with diabetes. Fifty years later, coinciding with the anniversary of VE Day, these precious archives have come to light. They show us the small yet important part the ESU members and staff of the United Kingdom, United States and Dominions contributed to the war relief during the Second World War.

This is a characteristically modest conclusion. The 'many millions' of items donated by the US and Dominions must have made a huge difference. They are a testament to the generosity of 'friends across the water'. The hospitality shown by the ESU was the best recompense that could be given. Young servicemen and women, far from home, could have a brief glimpse of happier times. Many of them must have gone on to make the ultimate sacrifice for freedom. From the ranks of ESU alumni alone, twenty Britons and four Americans gave their lives. On a happier note, a record 457 people attended a party at Dartmouth House held on 31 December 1945 to celebrate the end of the war.

There is an interesting coda to this story of the ESU at war. Back in 1939, at the commencement of hostilities, a young British barrister, with a thriving practice, laid it aside and put his highly-valued legal expertise at the disposal of his country. In 1946 he attended the Nuremberg trials of prominent Nazis. Deep friendships were forged with his American counterparts.

Decades later, those friendships had matured. The young barrister had gone on to serve his country in a variety of distinguished roles, culminating in being appointed British Ambassador to Washington. His expertise, together with American friendships forged at Nuremberg and afterwards, helped to secure a much-needed climate of goodwill for the ESU in a financially challenging time in the 1970s. The example of Sir Patrick Dean, former Chairman of the ESU, is a reminder that even the most harrowing of circumstances can carry the seeds of eventual good.

5
A Royal Friendship

'Many years ago, I became President of the English-Speaking Union of the Commonwealth and some years later I persuaded it to make the promotion of English, as an international language, its first priority.'
(HRH The Prince Philip, Duke of Edinburgh)

A fascinating royal *leitmotif* runs through the journey of the English-Speaking Union. We have seen how, as a young man attending the memorial service of Queen Victoria's eldest son, King Edward VII, in Westminster Abbey, Evelyn Wrench received his spiritual awakening. The upshot was the formation of firstly the Royal Over-Seas League and then the English-Speaking Union. In the last week of 1918, watching the meeting between President Wilson and King George V at Charing Cross railway station, Wrench felt that 'history was being made before my eyes'.

As we have seen, 1932 brought official recognition of Wrench's Herculean efforts in forming the ESU and helping to guide it through its first decade. He was knighted by King George V. There was a royal visit to Dartmouth House. A year later The Prince of Wales accepted the office of President. In 1937 King George VI granted the patronage of the British Empire to the ESU.

The royal connection continued with the 1941 visit to Dartmouth House by Queen Elizabeth to give support to the victims of war. After the war Princess Elizabeth, Duchess of Edinburgh, became President of the ESU. In 1952 Queen Elizabeth II became Patron and her husband, the Duke of Edinburgh, was invited to take over her role as President. At present The Queen and Prince Philip have been Patron and President respectively of the ESU for almost sixty years.

To be privileged to attend Buckingham Palace, enter the erstwhile sitting-room of King Edward VII and peruse the royal correspondence with the ESU is a veritable education. Prince Philip has given immense assistance to a wide variety of organisations. Nevertheless to read the correspondence is to leave oneself in no doubt whatsoever about the

ESU President's long-standing support for the progress of the English language in general and the ESU in particular. A few selected excerpts, taken over the years, may serve to illustrate.

In 1952, at the beginning of his patronage, Prince Philip, wrote, 'As President of the ESU of the Commonwealth, I am delighted to learn of the Union's plans for a major membership drive.' This membership drive was to ensure that the ESU could adequately serve the cause of comradeship between the peoples of the UK, the overseas Commonwealth and the US.

A forttieth celebration dinner for Sir Evelyn Wrench on 30 June 1958 elicited this approving message:

> The spectacular development and the prestige which the ESU enjoys today have their roots in Sir Evelyn's courage, foresight and unshaken belief in the cause to which he has devoted his life.
>
> Events in our lifetime have proved that the ideals for which the ESU stands were never of greater significance than they are today.

In the next year, 1959, the following letter was received from a Mr T.G.B. Lister from Leeds:

> As a teacher, I have had the privilege of serving in schools in Western Australia and England ...
>
> I believe there is a growing and fundamental need for the peoples of any one country to develop a closer and more tolerant understanding of the living conditions and ways of life of those in others.
>
> From my own small experience, I do know that in the school populations of England and Australia, there is a very blurred understanding of the other country and its way of life. Unfortunately this is sometimes so among even intelligent adults ...
>
> And I feel convinced that school ambassadors from one country to another, living and working away from home for a year, can become the links which will ultimately bind the Commonwealth even closer together.

This thoughtful, considered letter drew an equally thoughtful, considered reply directing its author to the ESU. In these easy days of 'credit card adventuring', it may be difficult for many to appreciate that post-war travel was far from easy. High journey costs, immigration restrictions and foreign exchange controls greatly impeded most people going abroad. It was particularly difficult for anyone without an official business reason to visit the dollar countries from the sterling countries. Nevertheless, as we will see, this was the era in which Lillian Moore and Yvonne Theobald, ESU Director and Assistant Director of Education respectively, were forging ahead so triumphantly with their education programmes.

On a lighter note, a couple of years later, in 1961, the following letter arrived from a Miss Pearl Milne from Edinburgh.

> Dear Sir,
> I have much pleasure in acknowledging receipt of the lovely tennis racquet kindly presented by H.R.H. The Duke of Edinburgh to the Edinburgh Branch of the ESU for their 'Thanksgiving Fair'. I was the lucky lady!

This drew the following response: 'His Royal Highness The Duke of Edinburgh asks me to thank you for your very courteous letter and to congratulate you on having won the prize.'

One senses a smile of delight, followed by a grave smile of approval. Hopefully the tennis racquet served its owner well for many years to come. Doubtless fellow players were charmed by its royal provenance.

In 1962 an ESU meeting was held at the Pacific Union Club in San Francisco to raise an appeal for Winston Churchill Travelling Fellowships. Present were Prince Philip and Lord Baillieu, ESU President and Chairman respectively.

> There will be established Winston Churchill Travelling Fellowships which will enable men and women in all parts of the Commonwealth and the United States to further their education in another part of the Commonwealth or the United States. The awards, which will be made without regard to race, colour, creed or social background, will not be confined to students or scholars in accredited institutions but will be open equally to those whose contributions to the community and their trade, industry, profession, business or calling would be increased through personal overseas study or travel.

Shortly afterwards, Miss Jane Moreland, a British exchange teacher who attended the ESU conference in San Francisco, wrote to the Director of the British Committee for the Interchange of Teachers in London. An extract from her letter reads thus:

I met wonderful people from all over the United States, Britain and the Commonwealth. The conference was an interesting one, especially the session on the Thursday at which His Royal Highness took the chair. I was very honoured and delighted to be presented to Prince Philip on two occasions. Everyone, and the Americans especially, I think, was most impressed with his charm, his wit and his obvious keen intelligence. I can honestly say, irrespective of who he is, that I have never attended a session which was presided over by a more capable chairman. Several Americans told me that they would like to borrow him for a while!

1963 saw Lord Baillieu considering his retirement as Chairman . He had served the ESU loyally since 1951. A tentative query regarding a possible future Chairman of the ESU, 'with fire in his belly', received the royal seal of approval, 'Excellent idea.'

The same year saw news of an ESU success story from Canada: 'You will be interested to know that membership of the Montreal branch of the ESU is now in excess of two thousand, which, after London, makes us the largest branch in the Commonwealth.' The prompt response was suitably appreciative: 'Delighted to hear Montreal branch of the ESU is doing so well. Keep it up.'

In the autumn of 1963 the American ESU was pondering its choice of a future Chairman (its equivalent of President). An approach to Prince Philip received the polite but firm admonition that 'It's the Americans' business.' There was no notion of British interference in any way whatsoever. The eventual choice was the former American President Eisenhower. With warmth, Prince Philip wrote: 'Delighted to know you have accepted Chairmanship of the ESU. This news will be received with great pleasure by all branches of the ESU of the Commonwealth.'

And then came the dreadful day of 22 November 1963, President Kennedy's assassination. Shortly afterwards, Prince Philip received the following poignant letter from D.D. Eisenhower, Chairman, and J.W.F. Treadwell, Vice-President of the English-Speaking Union of the United States.

Sir,

I have the honour to transmit to you a Resolution passed by the Executive Committee of the National Board of Directors of the ESU of the United States at their meeting held here on the sixteenth of December.

Let me add that, in such dark hours, the friendship that unites the English-Speaking peoples takes on a deeper significance as we find consolation in the knowledge that others understand and share our grief.

Sincerely,
Dwight D. Eisenhower

The ESU of the United States

December 30 1963

BE IT RESOLVED

That the Board of Directors of the ESU of the US hereby expresses to the ESU of the Commonwealth its most heartfelt appreciation of the many warm expressions of sympathy received from members and friends in Great Britain and other Commonwealth nations upon the death of John Fitzgerald Kennedy, President of the US.

Approved by unanimous vote of the executive Committee of the National Board of Directors of the English-Speaking Union of the US at its meeting, December 16th, 1963.

Hartley E. Howe
Acting Secretary

With the assassination of President Kennedy, there was a sense that not only America but the entire world had lost a great and much-needed man. For the rest of their lives millions of people would remember the moment when they first heard the fateful news. But life must go on. We owe it to the dead – and to the living. The 1964 National Conference of the ESU of the US was to be held in Denver. Prince Philip received a letter from Mr James S. Holme, President (the equivalent of Director-General) of the ESU of the US.

We have selected as the theme of the program of the Conference 'Four Hundred Years of English Language, Drama and Literature Since Shakespeare'.

In this connection, we are very eager to obtain the services of one of the world's leading interpreters of Shakespeare.

It was suggested to Mr Holme that Sir Laurence Olivier be contacted for advice as to who might be suitable. It appears that, somewhere along the way, wires became crossed and Sir Laurence, who was already committed to other projects, was forced to point out his ineligibility. This prompted the royal suggestion that, as it was only *advice* that was being sought, perhaps another approach was merited. The second approach was much more successful and Sir Laurence reported: 'I know that Sir Ralph Richardson will be out of the country on tour until August, and I would suggest that you contact Sir John Gielgud or Sir Alec Guinness.' One must agree with the royal verdict. 'This is a lot more useful!'

The Canadian ESU success story continued unabated, with the receipt of the following telegram:

> Pleased to report Montreal branch ESU has doubled membership since last cable, June, 1963. Membership now four thousand, making Montreal world's largest branch after London and New York. Hope you will address us when next in Canada.

By return post came: 'Delighted to hear that you have doubled your membership. Well done.'

On 24 January 1965 Winston Churchill died. The following day Lord Baillieu, Chairman of the English-Speaking Union of the Commonwealth, paid tribute to this distinguished statesman and war leader who had joined the ESU at its creation and was its Deputy-President at the time of his death. Lord Baillieu wrote:

> The valiant spirit of Winston Churchill is at rest. He loved life. He loved honour. He loved his country. When the world was shattered by the odious Nazi tyranny, he stood in the breach.
>
> In words heroic and inspired, in action, unceasing and defiant, he rallied his people and the free world for the battle. He charted the course of victory and he achieved with our Allies a triumph, overwhelming and complete.
>
> Great causes upheld him and moved him through his life.
>
> His name and fame will live forever among the immortals and, whenever men prize honour, virtue and courage, his story will be sung down the unending years to come.
>
> May he rest in peace and may we, in difficult days, take strength from the example of his life, his faith and his purpose.

For nearly fifty years Winston Churchill had been a loyal friend of the English-Speaking Union. As we shall later see, he was also visionary in his conception of the English language as a *lingua franca* for the entire world. He is owed a tremendous debt for his war leadership. Without his moral strength, much of Europe might have come to resemble a vast gulag. In his work and by the example of his life, he has bequeathed us a lesson in how an individual can profoundly affect history for the better. Throughout this book, we speak of 'multipliers', those with the power to influence others. Winston Churchill was the twentieth century's multiplier *par excellence*.

Less than two years afterwards came another obituary. One turns from the copy of Lord Baillieu's tribute to Winston Churchill in the royal correspondence to a newspaper cutting neatly affixed. It is from the *Daily Telegraph* of 12 November 1966. It is an obituary, entitled simply 'Sir Evelyn Wrench, man of friendship'. With mixed emotions of sadness and pride, one reads of the formation of the Royal Over-Seas Club (1910), the ESU (1918) and the All Peoples' Association (1930), 'which had, as its large object, the promotion of friendship among the peoples of the world'.

> He told in *Uphill*, the first volume of his autobiography, how, in 1910, a turning-point came in his life, crystallising itself in his memory as a 'vision' which came to him at the memorial service to King Edward VII in Westminster Abbey, where he said, 'the scales fell from my eyes. I vowed I would devote my life to great causes – to the Empire, to my fellows.'

How poignant to read these words in King Edward VII's former sitting room amid the correspondence of such a long-standing royal supporter of the ESU. The obituary lists Wrench's many honours: his chairmanship of *The Spectator* (he was a former editor), his 1932 knighthood, his Knight Commander (KCMG) award of 1960 and his 1964 Benjamin Franklin Award 'for his work for Anglo-American understanding', given by the Royal Society of Arts. Rightly he was lauded as 'a man of immense energy'.

It is more than a pity that Sir Evelyn Wrench was not able to witness the ESU's 1968 celebrations which would have given him especial pleasure. Lord Smallpiece wrote the following telegram to Prince Philip: 'In celebrating the Golden Jubilee of the ESU, members send their loyal greetings to your Royal Highness and offer their grateful thanks for the honour of your presidency.'

The simple, dignified reply conveyed a wealth of emotion. 'Thank you very much for your kind message. It has always given me the greatest pleasure to be your President.'

The 1960s had also seen the death of the renowned American statesman Adlai Stevenson. In 1970 a letter was received from Lady Benson:

> After Adlai Stevenson's death, my husband Rex Benson had the idea of making a small memorial library in his name in the ESU. He has given the bookcase and it was part of the idea that Adlai's friends be asked to fill it by donating a volume, grave or gay, which would have given Adlai pleasure.
>
> I do so hope that H.R.H. will honour us by contributing a book to the memorial library.

This prompted the modest (internal) response: 'The only thing I can think of is to offer copies of the two books of my speeches but you might enquire tactfully whether this would be appropriate or acceptable.'

As it happened, Lady Benson was delighted: 'We are naturally so pleased to receive your good news that Prince Philip will be contributing his books of speeches to the Adlai Stevenson memorial library.'

The 1970s will always be remembered as a time of political turmoil and economic hardship. As with other organisations, in both public and private sectors, the ESU was buffeted by the forces of recession and rampant inflation. Triumphantly it came through. At a banquet in the Connaught Rooms in London in 1974, to celebrate a revived English-Speaking Union, the dining room was filled with eminent figures. As guest of honour, Prince Philip summed up the proceedings thus:

> Well, ladies and gentlemen, I hope you have all enjoyed a pleasant evening. Because, starting tomorrow, I expect you all to redouble your efforts to make all the work and activities of the English-Speaking Union more effective and to give the Union greater influence.

At that banquet, both the President and the then Chairman of the ESU, Sir Patrick Dean, referred to the potential gap between mere communication and true understanding. Their remarks were highly appropriate to the fraught world of the 1970s energy crisis, when international relations were profoundly strained. However, these remarks are no less relevant to our modern world of so-called 'instant communication'.

First came a royal caution:

> The ability to communicate is not enough in itself. More important is the content of the messages which a common language allows to pass between us. It is, come to think of it, just as easy to curse someone in English as it is to bless him.

With his vast experience of international diplomacy, Sir Patrick continued this theme: 'Instant communication does not necessarily carry instant understanding. As often as not it leads to the reverse.'

Thirty-five years after these remarks were made at the launch of the 'new English-Speaking Union' in 1974, there is a sense of both prescience and resonance. English, as a shared language for the peoples of the world, is an admirable start. But, more than anything, what we really need is shared understanding of our problems and potentialities. Such shared understanding requires both comprehension and celebration of our diverse cultures. These, in turn, require a history of discourse. Thus the crucial importance of ESU exchange visits. In making their remarks, both the President and Chairman were underwriting the importance of the ESU's educational programmes in the last quarter of the twentieth century and beyond.

The 1970s saw a fascinating correspondence between Prince Philip and Sir James Pitman regarding simplified methods of teaching English. The adoption of English as a second language was becoming highly desired. Obviously the easier it is to learn English, the more people will be encouraged.

The IATEFL (International Association for the Teaching of English as a Foreign Language) held a conference in 1977. Prince Philip produced the following contribution:

> There is an obvious practical need for a common language for international communication – Greek, Latin and French have served various geographical areas at different times in history. Today it is not just a few linguistic groups in Europe and the Near-East but the whole world which requires to be able to communicate in a common language.
>
> English is already used by more non-natives than any other major language. Furthermore, as a consequence, so many of the technological and scientific advances having been made in English-speaking countries, a great many of the technical terms in use throughout the world have their origins in English. In some instances it has already been adopted – for example, by

international convention, English is used by Air Traffic Control throughout the world.

The 1970s saw terms such as 'youth unemployment' and 'graduate unemployment' come into general use for the first time. The 1950s and 1960s had comprised an era when, in the words of the former prime minister Harold Macmillan, 'Most of our people have never had it so good.' Contrary to popular perception, Macmillan made this remark in no spirit of complacency; instead he pondered whether such a favourable situation would continue. It did not. Writing to Sir Patrick Dean, Chairman of the ESU, from Windsor Castle in 1982, Prince Philip made a percipient comment: 'While I fully agree that there is a serious gap between school and employment, I just wonder whether the causes of this fairly recent phenomenon have been properly identified?'

Throughout the following decades, the oft-fraught relationship between education and employment would become of increasing concern. Education would be overhauled again and again. Looking backwards across some thirty years of educational endeavour, few would argue with another, modestly phrased comment from the same letter: 'Furthermore, I have a feeling that in recent years so much time and thought has gone into the structure of education that hardly any thought has been given to the content of education.'

Ironically, while devoted educationalists would concern themselves increasingly with the structure of their profession, with the liberalisation of the 1960s and 1970s, it sometimes seemed as though the structure of society itself was in danger of meltdown. In his letter to Sir Patrick, Prince Philip pinpointed another worrying facet of changing social structures: 'Academic standards may have slipped a bit but much more worrying is the very steep rise in juvenile crime.'

How do we best promote a society where people can discover and develop their talents? The question is one which continues to vex armies of educationalists and social commentators. One way is to create opportunities for civilised discourse where participants, in questioning others, inevitably learn to question themselves and their own cultural frameworks. Socrates was adamant that 'The unexamined life is not worth living'. For us to develop, we need to learn to examine our lives. Whether through reflection or discourse, language is our prime mode of expression. The ESU's promotion of debating and public speaking contests for young people at formative stages in their lives has had a huge impact upon thousands of people who would never otherwise have met. Cultural enclaves can become cultural prisons. In the twenty-first century, none of us can afford to live in cultural prisons.

1983 marked the end of Sir Patrick Dean's chairmanship of the ESU – although both he and his wife, Lady Dean, an ESU Governor, continued to be the most staunch of supporters. In a letter to Sir Patrick on 15 November 1982, Prince Philip commented: 'There is no doubt that the Union has taken a new lease of life and a new and a more appropriate direction under your leadership which I am sure is fully recognised by the membership.'

Sir Patrick's ten-year chairmanship of the ESU had come at the most difficult of times. No organisation, whether commercial or otherwise, will get through ninety years of life without encountering the odd 'sticky' patch. 1970s' recession and rampant inflation had proved the death knell for a myriad organisations. Sir Patrick had helped to deploy a range of ESU talent, from members, staff and governors, to steer the ESU successfully through distinctly choppy waters.

One of the major problems of the 1970s had been whether the ESU should sell Dartmouth House, to release capital and unburden itself of debt. For some, loss of Dartmouth House was tantamount to losing the spirit of the ESU; for others, it was a pragmatic option, however unpalatable. Sir Donald Tebbit, the incoming Chairman, wrote to his President of continuing *angst* regarding Dartmouth House. Alan Lee Williams, the then Director-General, liaised with Sir Hugh Jones, a former Director-General. Acting as a consultant to the ESU and intimately familiar with the problem from his own tenure as Director-General, Sir Hugh produced a 'comprehensive survey of the various options'. The Chairman commented, 'Sir Hugh rightly describes the loss of D.H. as "traumatic".'

A 1985 copy of a letter from Sir Donald Tebbit, regarding the proposed sale of Dartmouth House, further notes:

> Naturally there will be regret at the departure from Dartmouth House, a place which many have come to love. But by moving to a new home the object is to reinforce our business and to make a more balanced use of our assets, physical and financial.

A contemporary press release put the bravest possible face on impending events:

> Sir Donald Tebbit, Chairman of the E.S.U., said today 'We want to be able to plan for a period of secure expansion for the Union in the work for which we are best and even uniquely fitted. It is no easy matter to leave a Headquarters of which we are so fond and which has such historical associations, but in the last decade our work has grown vigorously in scope and variety and the Governors believe that we must mobilise our resources to best advantage in order to underpin it.'

For Prince Philip, who had given thirty years of service to the ESU by then, such correspondence, while unfortunately necessary, must have been deeply painful. And yet his mailbag was nothing if not varied. A 1985 letter, handwritten, in wonderfully flowing loops, by a Mr Ted W. Culp, from Toronto, vigorously proposed a case for simplified spelling.

> I ask yu tu suport publicly simplified spelling, and tu ask all Britons tu adopt it ... I also ask you tu join The S.S.S. [the Simplified Spelling Society – Mr Culp was its President] and tu becum activ in it ... I sujest that our English speling iz now such an incredibly erratic mess that it can be rationalized only in fazes. Speling reformasion iz inevitable and it iz desperately needed now.
>
> (Ted W. Culp, President S.S.S.)

Mr Culp was promptly thanked for his letter and received the following reply: 'On the subject of Simplified Spelling, your letter has been sent to the English-Speaking Union for their information.'

David Hicks, the Director of Education and a future Director-General of the ESU, as promptly wrote back, 'Once again many thanks for keeping me in the picture and I will certainly pass on Mr Culp's ideas to my language committee.'

In the same year, Michael Wynne-Parker, Vice-President E.S.U. of Sri Lanka, sent a brief note: 'I am enclosing a copy of the latest edition of *Open Mind*, the newspaper of the English-Speaking Union of Sri Lanka, which may interest His Royal Highness.'

This received the enthusiastic approval of Prince Philip, who had clearly enjoyed reading it. 'Splendid article about the cricket tests!'

In June 1986 David Hicks wrote regarding a BBC English Language Series, *The Story of English*:

> ... it leaves no one in any doubt that English is already the *lingua franca* of the world. It also stresses the number of changes

> taking place all the time to words, expressions and grammar, and the adaptability of English to new influences.

In 'The ESU and Globalisation' we explore the surge in globalisation at the end of the 20th century and beyond. Already the '*lingua franca*', English was poised to become a much prized 'cultural passport' for country after country seeking entry onto the world stage.

In August 1986 Alan Lee Williams left the ESU to become Warden and Chief Executive of Toynbee Hall. He had served over six years at the helm. The property issue had been resolved (once again) with Dartmouth House being saved (once again). As with so many, before and since, Alan Lee Williams has remained a good friend of the ESU. His gentle, self-effacing yet erudite manner is very much in keeping with the ethos of the English-Speaking Union.

In a letter to Sir Brian McGrath, Private Secretary to Prince Philip, Alan Lee Williams wrote: 'At a personal level, may I say how much I have enjoyed working with you and your staff and how much the fact that we have a President who takes a genuine interest in our English language side has been of immeasurable assistance to our educational work.'

The outgoing Director-General's report to NCEW (National Committee for England and Wales) in November 1986 was a typically thoughtful consideration of the complementary roles of Chairman and Director-General. It was – again typically thoughtfully – copied to the President.

> Mr Lee Williams said that although the Director-General is the chief spokesman, he is not the captain of the ship, that is the role of the Chairman. The Director-General is the pilot and if the captain and pilot do not work together the ship will soon be on the rocks. He was pleased to report that his relations with the two chairmen he had served under had avoided the rocks, but it always required, and will continue to require, delicate navigation.

The incoming Director-General, Rear-Admiral Richard Heaslip, received a typically warm welcome:

> Thank you for your letter and welcome to a different, but what I am sure will be a very rewarding job. I wish you every success.
>
> There is undoubtedly an awful lot for the ESU to do, but the problem is always to find the necessary financial resources.

A 1986 missive from an American ESU member, Dillon Ripley, from the delightfully named Paddling Ponds, Connecticut – seemingly an oasis of tranquillity – received the courteous reply, 'Thank you very much for your letter. You make me feel positively envious.'

An August 1986 letter from Sir Donald Tebbit contained official notification of the outcome of the 'property question'. 'The Governors therefore decided yesterday that we must remain in Dartmouth House and take the steps which are necessary to uplift it and to raise the funds we need.'

Stoicism on the part of the governors was rewarded by enhanced prospects for the ESU, as another August 1986 letter from Sir Donald Tebbit to Regional and Branch Chairmen (and copied to the President) reveals:

> Over the last year or so I have become more than ever convinced that the English-Speaking Union is even more necessary now than it was in the past. The phenomenal growth of the English language and the speeding up of communication and travel in the world give us immense opportunities. Our constitutional purpose of working for friendship between peoples has an ever-widening scope as is shown by the foundation of new branches all over the world.

In 1989 another fundamental issue arose, this time about the naming and identity of the ESU. Lord Pym, who was now the Chairman, wrote:

THE ENGLISH-SPEAKING UNION AND THE COMMONWEALTH

> We were established in 1918 as 'The English-Speaking Union', a title which lasted until 1952 when it was changed to 'The English-Speaking Union of the Commonwealth'. The name is enshrined in our Royal Charter; any change needs the assent of the Privy Council.
>
> The new name reflected Britain's withdrawal from Empire, and also the make up of the ESU, which apart from the United States was composed at that time entirely of Commonwealth countries.
>
> Since then, the emergence of English as the World language has widened the spread of the ESU. Europe is now the fastest growth area, with ESU branches in Brussels, Munich, Schaffhausen and most recently Paris, and serious prospects in Vienna, Helsinki, Venice and Budapest. They find that the ESU is a pleasant and

productive way to get to grips with the English-speaking world without any accompanying political overtones.

Dartmouth House is looked to for leadership, but the Commonwealth title is now unduly restricting and can cause misunderstandings in Europe. A fitting change would be to revert to our time-honoured title of 'The English-Speaking Union' which, like the titles of 'The Royal Navy' and 'The Royal Mail', would indicate our pre-eminence as the founding ESU without any geographical limitations.

It is intended to approach the Privy Council along these lines.

Lord Pym, visiting the Palace on this issue, received a most sympathetic hearing. However, a less sympathetic public hearing delivered a resounding verdict in favour of the status quo. A 1990 letter from Lord Pym, regarding 'The Title of the ESU', recorded: 'At the Extraordinary General meeting last week, required to be held under our constitution, the proposal to revert to our original title of the "English-Speaking Union" was not carried.' A 75% majority was needed; opponents turned up in sufficient numbers to block it.

From another letter at this time, on one issue, the President was resolute. The ESU's future was about far more than mere survival. While entirely affably couched, the intention could not be more clear. And indeed, with the collapse of the Berlin Wall in 1989, new countries were entering the international community. Looking back over two decades, one can now see that the President's exhortation was perfectly timed. By responding so well to a hitherto undreamed-of opportunity, the ESU thrived beyond anybody's wildest expectations.

At the beginning of the last decade of the twentieth century, there was a change of leadership in the ESU. David Hicks, formerly Head of Education, became Director-General and Valerie Mitchell, previously Director of Branches and Cultural Affairs, was promoted to Deputy Director-General.

For the English-Speaking Union of the United States of America, 1990 was a very special year. From Buckingham Palace, Brigadier Clive Robertson, wrote: 'I now enclose The Duke of Edinburgh's signed message for the ESU-USA National Council Meeting in Atlanta in October.'

I hope that all members of the English-Speaking Union of the Commonwealth join me in offering our warmest congratulations to the English-Speaking Union of the United States of America on reaching its 70th anniversary.

The world has changed in many ways since Sir Evelyn Wrench founded the ESU and I am sure that he would have approved the present emphasis on the promotion of the English language as a means of creating international understanding and goodwill.

Your work in helping people throughout the world to learn English through your Excellence in English, English in Action, Shakespeare and literacy programs and your travel and study schemes is much admired and I am quite sure that it is making a significant contribution to friendship and the exchange of ideas across all boundaries.

The 1990s would see much discussion about the value of competition in education. Regarding the 1991 World Schools Debating Championships in Edinburgh, Prince Philip had this to say: 'There are bound to be winners and losers in any contest, but I hope that all the competitors will go home with respect for their opponents and with the realisation that different opinions are no bar to lasting friendships.'

One trusts that the participants of these and of so many other debating contests sponsored by the ESU have gone home not only with respect for their opponents but with a greater realisation of the power that personal development has to change so many lives – not just your life but the lives of all with whom you come in contact.

1991 saw an exhortation of the roles of the ESU in general and its George Washington Ball in particular.

A common language is the priceless asset of the English-speaking peoples of the world. The English-Speaking Union was founded to make use of that asset in furthering goodwill and understanding between the English-speaking nations. Since then English has become the most widely used second language all over the world. This development is warmly welcomed by the ESU which believes that understanding depends on good communication and works to nurture and expand the use of the English language.

The purpose of the George Washington Ball is to give pleasure to all the guests, but it is also to give them the opportunity to feel righteous at the same time by making a contribution towards the George Washington Business Scholarships and the Evelyn Wrench Awards.

Every single ESU activity is underpinned by the role of language in communication and subsequent relationship building. As a 1992 letter made clear:

> Language is an important part of every national culture. Although scientists and others have made use of a common language for many years, the advent of voice radio has brought a new dimension to international communication. It has created a practical necessity for people with different languages to be able to communicate with one another for technical purposes. Air traffic controllers were the first to introduce a system of standard words and phrases ...

In the same year, a letter from Balmoral, regarding the forthcoming World Members Conference meeting in Washington DC, continued this theme:

> Many members of my generation fondly believed that the end of the Second World War would usher in a new age of peace, humanity and prosperity. Instead, the last fifty years have brought a succession of racial, civil, religious and ideological conflicts of horrific brutality in almost every sector of the globe.
>
> It is, of course, possible to use a common means of communication to hurl insults and to promote division and resentment, but without a common language, there would be even less hope of negotiation, compromise and reconciliation.
>
> The English-Speaking Union was formed to promote understanding and friendship between people who shared the same language. It then became apparent that, by promoting the use of English as a common language, it would be helping all people to understand each other and to encourage friendship, trade and cultural exchanges. It would also give them a better chance to discuss and to resolve their differences.

A coda to these remarks, in December 1992, reflects: 'Many years ago, I became President of the English-Speaking Union of the Commonwealth and some years later I persuaded it to make the promotion of English, as an international language, its first priority.'

As has previously been mentioned, in the late 1970s the BBC produced a series entitled *The Story of English*. A 1993 letter, written by Prince Philip from Windsor Castle, commented:

> This special edition of *The Story of English* has been produced to mark the 75th anniversary of the founding of the English-Speaking Union in 1918. The founder, Sir Evelyn Wrench, saw it as 'A movement to draw together in the bonds of comradeship the English-speaking peoples of the world'. That was his vision, but I wonder whether he ever dreamed of the rate at which the use of English has spread in recent years. It is estimated to have become the first or the preferred foreign language of a billion people throughout the world.
>
> Quite apart from the opportunity to enjoy the rich cultural heritage of the English language, it now also provides a means of direct communication for people involved in science, technology, business, trade and travel. Special versions of English have also been developed for particular purposes, such as traffic control in the air and at sea, international police work and international military communication.

A further letter, written from Buckingham Palace in 1993, noted:

> The ability to communicate is the one great advantage that the human species has over all others, but different languages still act as barriers and prevent the wider exchange of views and ideas. English-speaking people have taken their language to many parts of the globe and for the last 75 years the English-Speaking Union has been promoting friendly relations and encouraging contacts between these widely dispersed communities. In more recent years it has been active in encouraging the use of English as a second language all over the world.

A letter written at the end of 1994 to the ESU of the US for its forthcoming 75th Anniversary celebrations mused:

> It is not all that easy to start something, but a good idea at one point in history may not be such a good idea when circumstances change. The great thing about Sir Evelyn Wrench's idea is that it was relevant at the time it was conceived and it has remained relevant ever since. Even then a good idea cannot flourish by itself, it needs the vision and commitment of loyal supporters, who alone can ensure that it will continue to achieve its founder's ambitions.
>
> I am quite convinced that the growing number of English-Speaking Union branches round the world are making an

> increasingly important contribution to international understanding and goodwill. I have no doubt that Sir Evelyn would be pleased with the way his idea is developing.

By this time, to meet a global need, the ESU was expanding dramatically. Evelyn Wrench's vision was being transmitted all over the world. A 1997 letter from Buckingham Palace praised its hosting of the first International Council meeting in Asia:

> There has always been a need for traders, business people, scientists, scholars and many others to communicate across language barriers. Now that the world has become a global village, the need for a common means of communication is greater than ever. For a number of historical reasons, the use of the English language has been spreading around the world and is now being recognised as the most convenient form of international communication.
>
> The English-Speaking Union recognised this trend many years ago and has become actively engaged in the promotion of the language as a means of practical communication between people across the world.
>
> I am delighted that the English-Speaking Union of Pakistan has persuaded the International Council of the English-Speaking Union to meet in Karachi to coincide with the celebration of Pakistan's Golden Jubilee. This will be its first meeting in Asia and it recognises the extensive use of the language in this very densely populated and economically active part of the world. I am sure the meeting will be a great success and that the members of the Council will thoroughly enjoy the hospitality of their hosts.

Much of the 1990s expansion of the ESU had been spearheaded by Baroness Brigstocke as Chairman and Valerie Mitchell as Director-General. As the millennium approached, Baroness Brigstocke approached the end of her tenure. On 16 November 1999, Prince Philip gracefully acknowledged her distinctive contribution:

> Dear Lady Brigstocke,
>
> Word has reached me that you will be retiring as Chairman of the ESU in the near future. I know that everyone connected with ESU will be very sad indeed to see you go. Many people have given great service to the organisation, but I can say with all truthfulness that no Chairman in my time has been more dedicated or

done more to encourage and promote the ESU than you have over the last six years.

You have stimulated a dramatic growth in the organisation in spite of some quite daunting financial constraints and I hope you will accept this very sincere expression of thanks and appreciation on behalf of everyone in the English-Speaking Union of the Commonwealth.

Yours sincerely,
Philip

Prince Philip has continued his loyal service to the English-Speaking Union throughout the first decade of the twenty-first century. To give such generous support for well-nigh sixty years is no small matter – especially when you are one of the busiest and most sought-after men in the world. To visit Buckingham Palace and peruse nearly sixty years of correspondence is an emotional experience. One comes away with no possible doubt of the depth of friendship. Unlike so much in life, friendship is a true gift; it is either given freely or it is not given at all. The English-Speaking Union has been greatly favoured and is deeply honoured. No organisation has ever had a more steadfast royal friend.

6
ESU Educational Programmes and Awards

'The ESU is, above all, a place for ideas.' (Belinda Norman-Butler)

For almost ninety years the English-Speaking Union has run a wide variety of educational programmes in different countries and in different continents. All of these programmes have a common aim: to deliver educational benefit to those most likely to use it to maximum advantage. On completion of a programme, every scholar automatically becomes a privileged ESU alumnus. By using their ESU-inspired educational gains in their careers and in inspiring others, ESU alumni, 'the leaders of tomorrow', maximise the outcomes. In our twenty-first century 'Information Age', investing in our personal and career development is probably the soundest investment that any of us can make. Investing in the personal and career development of tomorrow's leaders – and world leaders – is probably the soundest investment any society can make. The following examples demonstrate the depth, breadth and longevity of ESU programmes and awards, so highly respected all around the world.

THE ENGLISH-SPEAKING UNION DUKE OF EDINBURGH ENGLISH LANGUAGE BOOK AWARD

This was founded in 1971 to recognise the best book published each year in the field of English language teaching and learning. A single winning work and two runners-up are selected on the basis of originality, innovation and substance. It is a major award, with over fifty publishers invited to enter. For many years the distinguished judging panel has been chaired by the eminent grammarian Lord Quirk. The authors and publishers of the winning entry and the two highly commended works take part in a ceremony at Buckingham Palace. The awards are presented personally by the President of the English-Speaking Union, the Duke of Edinburgh. The results are widely reported in the press, professional journals and ESU communications. The winner and runners-up may use the ESU logo and acknowledgement or commendation.

To make learning accessible and enjoyable, it is necessary to *engage* the learner. Obviously the more accessible, the more enjoyable, the easier we make the learning of English, the more people will be encouraged to do it. A trawl through comments made about recent entrants and winners of the English Language Book Award revels a theme of *engagement* in learning.

> 'clever, economical, engaging and fun ...'

> 'a quirky, humorous style ...'

> 'all-encompassing, impressively lucid and extensively researched ...'

> 'a wonderful resource, showing a clear link between theory and practice, with some excellent tasks, as well as being easy for the teacher to use.'

> 'it has hammered a post in the ground as to the current thinking and practice in English Language teaching ...'

For an author, receiving this award is a tremendous accolade. A recent winner, Alison Waters, from the ELT department of the Oxford University Press, commented:

> My colleagues and I enjoyed the day very much. It was a great privilege to be awarded the ESU prize jointly with OUP USA and receiving the award from Prince Philip in Buckingham Palace was especially exciting. Having the *Oxford Students' Dictionary* recognised in this way makes us very proud of our editorial efforts and being able to chat to Prince Philip about it and meet other authors and publishers who were also receiving awards made the ceremony very special indeed.

THE ESU PRESIDENT'S AWARD

This was inaugurated in 2003 at the request of the ESU President, HRH The Duke of Edinburgh. It is given annually for innovation in the use of new technologies, such as CD-ROMs and websites, to enhance English teaching and learning worldwide. It thus builds on the success of The English Language Book Award. It follows a similar judging process. Once again the winners have the chance to visit Buckingham Palace and receive their awards personally from the Duke of Edinburgh. Again there is the theme of *engagement* – of using technologies unknown to previous generations, to enable the teaching and learning of English to be accessible and enjoyable.

> 'children found the CD-ROM to be cool, exciting and interesting ...'
>
> 'opened up an imaginary world for young ELT learners through music and design ...'
>
> 'fun, vital and visually exciting ...'
>
> 'taking children to new imaginary worlds and allowing them to engage in learning through exploration ...'

In the words of the Duke of Edinburgh: 'Many years ago, I became President of the English-Speaking Union of the Commonwealth and some years later I persuaded it to make the promotion of English, as an international language, its first priority.'

The English-Speaking Union Duke of Edinburgh English Language Book Award and the ESU President's Award are uniquely positioned to stimulate the production of better and better teaching and learning material. It is a winning formula in which everyone benefits: the learner, the teacher, the writer and the publisher. These awards bear vivid testimony to the capability, dedication and staying power of many people, particularly the Duke of Edinburgh and Lord Quirk.

THE WALTER HINES PAGE TRAVELLING SCHOLARSHIP, THE SCHOOLBOY EXCHANGE SCHEME, THE BRITISH MOREHEAD-CAIN SCHOLARSHIP AND THE CHAUTAUQUA BELL TOWER SCHOLARSHIP

From 1923 onwards, the Walter Hines Page Travelling Scholarship has made provision for British teachers and educators to work in the United States. Scholars travel to the USA to study a specific aspect of American education which interests them and which is relevant to their professional roles. They are given the opportunity to travel widely in the USA. Throughout their tours, these scholars are guests of branches of the English-Speaking Union of the United States. American ESU members arrange the programmes based around professional contacts made by the scholars prior to the visit. The result is twofold: professional development of the educator and a furthering of the exchange of professional ideas between the US and the UK.

Five years after the inception of the Walter Hines Page Scholarship, a chance meeting arose between the Warden of Radley College near Oxford and the Headmaster of Tabor Academy in Massachusetts. The latter was concerned about providing opportunities for children orphaned by the First World War. The conversation between the two headmasters resulted in the founding of another scholarship. The Schoolboy Exchange Scheme made it possible for British schoolboys to travel to America and spend a year in a US preparatory school. It was thus an annual pre-university scholarship. The British boys would meet at Dartmouth House before travelling to Tilbury to embark on their voyage across the Atlantic. No doubt the occasional tear was shed. The first tranche of schoolboys was chosen by an ESU selection committee and departed in September 1929. At the same time, three American schoolboys arrived from the US to attend school at Radley. The ESU had forged another key link.

The Schoolboy Exchange scheme has blossomed and, some eighty years later, many lives have been transformed by the experience of inhabiting another sympathetic culture at a formative age. Now known as The ESU Secondary Schools Exchange (SSE) scholarships, they are open to both boys and girls. Each year 25–30 students in the UK, of all backgrounds, are offered the opportunity to spend two or three terms at a private school in the USA or Canada. Students should be under 19½ years old, must have taken A-levels or equivalent, and must be intending to study at a UK university on their return. The scholarship covers the cost of tuition, board and lodging; all other costs are covered by the scholar. Scholars are placed in independent day and boarding schools across the US, such as Packer Collegiate Institute in New York and Lawrenceville School in New Jersey.

And the value in terms of personal development? In the words of Jasmine Rahman, a 2009/10 scholar at Culver Academy, Indiana: 'When I left Britain, the full implications of my time spent abroad did not occur to me. What I gained at Culver was far different from anything I had imagined. It was highly educational. This year has been a turning point in every aspect of my life.'

By contrast, the British Morehead-Cain Scholarships to the University of North Carolina at Chapel Hill provide up to four places each year, fully funded, for selected British school leavers to pursue a first-degree programme. All secondary schools in the United Kingdom are eligible to nominate students, who need to demonstrate outstanding achievement in leadership, scholarship, moral force of character and physical vigour. The Morehead-Cain is one of the world's most generous and prestigious university scholarships.

As we shall see, the history of the Chautauqua Bell Tower Scholarship has been memorably described by Will Glover in 'The Alumnus Experience'.

> A word too often used to describe Chautauqua is 'unique' and yet that is precisely what the institution is ... Chautauqua is an experience individual to each Chautauquan ... the chance for each and every voice to sing its song, to explore the symphony of your life ... Here, at Chautauqua, the scholar takes flight ...

As Will writes, 'clergy, knights of the realm, journalists, academics and headmasters' are just a few of the professional groups which have benefited. He was personally 'fortunate enough to become acquainted with industry, religious, political and world leaders'. Nobody can read his account without being deeply impressed by the power of the experience upon him and by what he has subsequently given back to society. It is clear that Chautauqua is a very special experience indeed.

BOOKS ACROSS THE SEA – AMBASSADORS OF GOODWILL

In 1941 there was a spate of Nazi radio propaganda aimed at driving a wedge between Anglo-American relations. Expatriate Americans who had remained in the UK (against their government's advice) hired Caxton Hall in Westminster and rallied fellow countrymen to help the war effort. They included three people who were to become pivotal to the struggle: Professor Arthur Newell, Beatrice Warde and Alicia Street. They wrote, lectured and broadcast, while also founding an organisation called the American Outpost in Britain. A dire lack of shipping space meant that transatlantic book transportation was severely impaired. The relatively few travellers would stuff a few volumes into already tightly packed suitcases but clearly this was a situation that needed to be rectified.

Accordingly Beatrice Warde found herself Chairman of the evocatively entitled 'Books Across the Sea' Committee. An American citizen, she had graduated from Barnard College, New York, in 1921. Her published research into the history and practice of typography led to a move to England when she was invited to join the staff at the Monotype Corporation of London in 1927. Monotype was a firm of established international prestige in the graphic arts. From 1927 onwards, Beatrice Warde became their publicity manager and editor of *The Monotype Recorder*.

Early in the Second World War Beatrice Warde established *The Token of Freedom*, a pocket anthology 'forming a spiritual passport fit to accompany the children of the defenders of freedom who set sail from Great Britain in 1940'. A copy was presented to all evacuees from the UK to America and Canada. She also established the Kinsman Association, bringing together evacuees' parents on this side of the Atlantic and the American foster parents on the other side, so that the children would maintain relationships with home.

Beatrice Warde's mother, May Lamberton Becker, was the literary editor of the *New York Herald Tribune*. As committed a British-American as her daughter, her American royalties from *Introducing Charles Dickens* (written in the first year of the Second World War) paid for the appropriately named 'Charles Dickens' ambulance in London. Her British royalties were spent on UK welfare projects.

She was therefore the perfect person for Beatrice Warde to enlist in her quest for books to be donated to the American Outpost for distribution in Britain. Mrs Becker published an appeal in the 'Readers' Guide' column of her newspaper and hundreds of readers voted for the most suitable titles. Initially seventy books, carefully selected to mirror life in the two countries, were chosen. Educational titles were particularly valued. The books were despatched to London and a reception was held, to which publishers, librarians and distinguished people of letters were invited. A plan was devised for a reciprocal collection to be sent to America. Accordingly two Books Across the Sea societies were formed. By the end of 1941, courtesy of these societies, there were over 1,000 more books on each side of the Atlantic. The respective branches also acted as inquiry centres about life in the two countries. *The Times* of 2 January 1942 contained an article by Beatrice Warde entitled 'Books Across the Sea; Ambassadors of Good Will'. Succinctly put.

Initially Professor Arthur Goodhart provided a home for books in the UK at his chambers in Lincoln's Inn. The poet T. S. Eliot, an American who had adopted British citizenship, was an inspired choice of Chairman of the British Books Across the Sea (BAS). In America, Dr Alan Nevins was President of the scheme and the books were housed in the Browsing Room at Columbia University in New York.

The two collections quickly outgrew their allotted spaces and new premises had to be found. In London, Lionel McColvin offered a special room at South Audley Street Public Library in Mayfair to house 2,400 volumes. This was opened by the US president's wife, Eleanor Roosevelt saying: 'We can't all visit each other, but at least let's read about each other.' A further 450 volumes were retained at Lincoln's Inn; in 1946 they were moved to a new office in Fetter Lane.

In his Presidential address to the BAS Society in January 1946, T. S. Eliot said:

> The need for closer reciprocal understanding is greater now than at any period in the past, and the lack of it would be more dangerous for the world. The work of BAS has become more important than it was during the war, when the difficulties were merely physical ones caused by the breakdown in communications. The next few years will be crucial, and it will be essential to maintain the spirit of co-operation.

To post-war generations 1946 can easily appear as a blessed 'peace in our time'. The reality was brutally different. Britain had been made well-nigh bankrupt by the war. Country after country was ruined. Untold millions had perished, many of them dreadfully. The wily Stalin had emerged victorious from the Yalta conference. World communism was the declared aim of the Soviet Union, and destabilisation of both western and eastern nations was the amorally pragmatic method of achieving it. The tragedy was that many indigenous communists were men and women of high morals and noble aspirations who genuinely believed that the Soviet Union was a sound model of the fairest possible society. Five minutes in a gulag would have convinced them otherwise.

So T. S. Eliot's words were deadly serious. Faced with the danger of communist world government – which would have been little different from Nazi world government – Anglo-American friction was an unaffordable luxury. Much of the Cold War between capitalism and communism would be fought in Europe, centred on Berlin. Above all, it would be a battle for hearts and minds, between truth and lies. Rightly, T. S. Eliot went on to suggest that readers on the Continent were starved of English language books. An exchange with Brussels was a beginning and exchanges were planned for other countries.

In 1948 the ESU in London and the ESU in New York invited the two BAS schemes to form new committees and, as accommodation gradually became available, libraries were created within both organisations. So Books Across the Sea found the most congenial of homes.

In 1960 Beatrice Warde founded the reading room in the National Book League's Library as a memorial to her mother, May Lamberton Becker. The room was opened by their old comrade, T. S. Eliot. In 1964 an article about Beatrice Warde was published in *The Times*. It was entitled 'Pioneer in a Man's World'. Subsequently the following letter appeared:

> Sir,
>
> Mrs Warde's many friends will have read with delight the article 'Pioneer in a Man's World' on February 10th in which a well-deserved and notable tribute is paid to her and her work as a specialist in the world of typography. The article touched on an aspect of Mrs Warde's extra-mural activities, the Anglo-American book exchange, of which she was co-founder, and on which I should like to add a few words. Those of us who have seen her in action know her remarkable enthusiasm and drive in leading the Books Across the Sea movement, which continues to flourish despite slender means under her Chairmanship, and is sponsored by the English-Speaking Union.
>
> There is no need to stress the continued importance of projects such as these for the extension of better knowledge and understanding.
>
> Yours faithfully
> Margaret Alexander of Tunis
> Joint Deputy Chairman, The English-Speaking Union

May Lamberton Becker died in 1958 and Beatrice Warde died in 1969. Both women were lovers of words and lovers of freedom. They gave so much when it was desperately needed. Happily, Alicia Street continued to work for the ESU for several decades to come.

Until 1984 children's books (for five to sixteen-year olds) from Britain were exchanged with America, Canada and Australia. The books were housed at the Walter Hines Page Memorial Library at Dartmouth House in London. However, due to a lack of space, the Library Committee of the ESU sought to donate the collection to an institution which would keep the books together. The University of Kent, as a corporate member of the English-Speaking Union, agreed to accept the collection which comprises some 511 non-fiction and fiction books. The Templeman Library has volumes on American history, on the different nationalities who emigrated there, on politics, natural history and music. The collection also contains a number of biographies and books of children's poetry.

In the English-Speaking Union of the United States, Books Across the Sea continues to flourish. The Ruth M. Shellens Memorial Library, in the ESU's National Headquarters in New York City, has more than 4,000 books about the history and culture of the UK. Ambassador Book Awards are made annually to authors whose works are adjudged to have made an exceptional contribution to interpreting the life and culture of the United States to other English-speaking people. These Ambassador books are sent to ESU branches overseas, so that they receive the widest possible dissemination. The inspiration of Beatrice Warde and May Lamberton Becker lives on.

LILLIAN MOORE AND YVONNE THEOBALD

No serious consideration of the history of the ESU's educational programmes is possible without paying tribute to the work of Lillian Moore and Yvonne Theobald, long-standing Head and Deputy Head respectively of the Education Department. Because these two worked so closely together for many years, it is appropriate to consider their contributions as a joint effort. Sadly Lillian Moore died in 1980; but, at the time of writing, Yvonne Theobald is still with us, actively enjoying her well-earned retirement. As with so many ESU staff, past and present, Yvonne is extremely modest about her contribution but, from in-depth interviewing, it is apparent that Lillian and she formed one of those rare 'dream teams' where both partners almost instinctively act in concert. So it is likely that much of what was written about Lillian applies almost equally to Yvonne.

Both joined the ESU in 1947 and made a great contribution to the Education Department during the following decades until Lillian's retirement in 1976 and Yvonne's retirement in 1989. As we have seen in 'The ESU at War', the dangers of the North Atlantic curtailed the UK/US exchange of students and the ESU changed its role firstly to that of an aid organisation and then to a hospitality organisation. Both these roles were of obvious importance to the war effort. Understandably, at the end of the war, renewed effort had to be put into the ESU's educational programmes. Lillian and Yvonne were scarcely working at normal jobs; theirs was an avocation, going far beyond the call of duty, with gruelling workloads and long hours to match. Often the selection committees comprised leading figures from the educational world; very often it was a stringent, daunting process. The world was then a much more formal place. With judgement and good humour, Lillian and Yvonne calmed, coached and cajoled thousands of schoolboys, schoolgirls, undergraduates, graduates and teachers. Many of these nervous applicants went on to become leading figures in commerce, industry, politics and the Civil Service. They repaid their freely given career investments by supporting the ESU in a variety of ways, such as donating money, suggesting applicants and serving on selection panels themselves. Thus Lillian and Yvonne built up a huge network of educationalists, scholars and professional contacts. The upshot? Everybody benefited. Present ESU programmes owe a tremendous debt to the work that Lillian and Yvonne did, all those years ago. After Lillian's retirement, Yvonne worked with David Hicks, the incoming Head of Department and subsequent ESU Director-General.

Hugh Jones, Director-General of the ESU in the 1970s, struck the right note: 'If Dartmouth House was the English-Speaking Union to the social world, Lillian Moore was the ESU to the education world. She had grown with the organisation from office assistant and won the gratitude and affection of thousands of beneficiaries over the years.'

Lillian's obituary in *Concord* paid tribute thus: 'Her administrative gifts, her remarkable memory and above all her capacity for friendship, understanding and sympathy made her the ideal person for the job to which she devoted her life.'

Of the myriad scholars who passed through their hands, Yvonne struggles to think of one who did not benefit significantly from their ESU programme. Of her forty-two years of ESU service, she says simply, 'From the moment I walked through the door of Dartmouth House, I knew that it was the right place for me.'

THE ESU MUSIC SCHOLARSHIPS

During the Second World War, a lady named Belinda Norman-Butler volunteered to help at the ESU's Cambridge Centre. Little did anyone realise that this was the beginning of a relationship which would span six decades. After the war she moved to London with her husband, joined the ESU's Education Committee and was appointed to the Board of Governors. 'I had a rough time,' she later candidly admitted. While she strongly approved of the then Chairman, Lord Baillieu, she felt that many other governors were businessmen and academics with little inclination for her abiding passion – music. When she proposed that Ralph Vaughan Williams and Benjamin Britten should be asked to become ESU Vice-Presidents, she was loftily rebuffed by an economist on the Board of Governors with 'We don't want any more of Mrs Norman-Butler's long-haired musicians!' The subject of his remarks tartly pointed out that, after all, Vaughan Williams was an OM, 'if you know what that means ...'

Undaunted, Belinda organised a series of exchange scholarships between young people in the UK and in the US, four each year from each country. As we have seen, this was a time when tight exchange controls prevented almost anyone from travelling to America except on business, to win dollar currency for Britain. British scholars were hosted by ESU members in the US while the American scholars were similarly hosted by ESU members in the UK. Two Americans were pivotal to the success of these scholarships: Frank Dobie, Professor of American History at Cambridge, and James Lawrence, chairman of the Boston branch which provided the first American hosts in 1948. Both became lifelong friends.

In 1953 Belinda organised her first concert for the ESU. It could scarcely have been a more memorable occasion, a performance of Handel's Messiah held in Westminster Abbey, so soon after the Queen's Coronation that the blue and gold furniture installed for the ceremony was still in place. The concert audience made good use of extra platforms which had been raised so that Coronation attendees could see and hear better. Reginald Jacques conducted the Bach Choir, of which Belinda was a member. The Jacques Orchestra was led by Emanuel Hurwitz, who was to serve on the ESU Music Scholarships adjudication panel for many decades.

In 1969 Belinda devised a scheme for ESU Music Scholarships and organised a concert at the Banqueting Hall in Whitehall for the visiting Boston Chamber Players. £1,500 was raised: a significant sum at that time. However she was scandalised when the ESU Governors tried to appropriate it for other schemes, rather than letting her use it for her music project. It seems that philistinism was still alive. Faced with such stern opposition, it took another three years and another concert at St John's, Smith Square, again with the Boston Players, to raise enough money to begin the scholarship scheme. Even then, advised by Sir Robert Mayer, she waited until a really outstanding young artist emerged before launching the first scholarship at Tanglewood, the most prestigious of the American summer schools of music. That young artist was a teenage violinist named Nigel Kennedy. The year was 1975. The following year Simon Rattle was nominated, only to be turned down, courtesy of a certain member of the adjudication panel.

Since 1975, thanks almost entirely to Belinda's energy in exploiting contacts, the scholarship list expanded beyond Tanglewood to include the other summer schools – Aspen, Banff, Yale and Rivinia. The list of scholars bears testament to the general success of the adjudication panel in spotting future stars such as Steven Isserlis, Robert Cohen, Tasmin Little, Lorraine McAslan, Grant Llewellyn, and Michael Collins. Loyally the scholars have subsequently given their services to the many concerts which Belinda organised in aid of the Scholarship Fund. Often the splendid orchestras of the Purcell School and the Menuhin School contributed.

Looking back over her decades of ESU service and remembering some of the arguments she had in committee with less imaginative colleagues, Belinda Norman-Butler briskly and boldly summed it up: 'The ESU is, above all, a place for ideas.' In 1996 she was awarded the Churchill Medal of Honour for her contribution to those ideas and for her long-standing commitment to putting them into practice.

Although in a wheelchair at her hundredth birthday concert, 'Belinda addressed the audience most warmly but sadly seemed to bid us farewell.' Just over two weeks later, on 26 December 2008, she died. Her *Times* obituary noted:

> Belinda Norman-Butler was both *femme formidable* and *grande dame*. ... on the one hand, a kind of radiant innocence; on the other, an irresistible authority, which might have been branded as bossiness but for her great charm.
>
> Until her late nineties she was to be seen at almost all literary societies and gatherings, bending her warm, eager gaze on the young, ready to be enlightened, entertained or amused, or to deliver a witty aside.

The ESU Music Scholarships are her legacy to all of us.

ENGLISH IN ACTION

With the English in Action scheme, the ESU owes a clear intellectual debt to the English-Speaking Union of the United States, particularly the New York branch which originated it. In 1994 Alison Wheatcroft, a former tutor in the American scheme, brought it to the UK. English in Action helps non-native English speakers to gain confidence and skills in understanding and speaking English. Students develop via weekly conversation practice with a tutor whose first language is English. In addition to practising their English, students learn about life in the United Kingdom and also teach their tutor about their own country and customs. (It's always good when teachers learn from their students.) Obviously students must have at least a basic knowledge of English in order to participate, although nearly two decades' experience attests that such knowledge will not remain basic for long. Tutors don't need any formal training but they do need to be good communicators with an interest in other languages and cultures and the commitment to provide language support to someone new to the UK. The programme currently attracts over 100 students annually and operates in three ten-week terms. In addition to 'creating global understanding through English', English in Action has proved an excellent recruiting medium and sparked many new friendships.

One intriguing offshoot of English in Action has been a programme for refugee children in primary schools to help improve their English language skills through informal means such as playing, singing, cooking and conversation. It will readily be appreciated that refugee children are among the most deserving of all. To arrive in a strange country and begin again is a daunting affair for anyone; to do so as a vulnerable, perhaps traumatised child must be doubly daunting. English in Action teams have found that imaginative, hands-on teaching helps these children become confident in understanding the complexities of a new language and a new culture. Today's refugee is tomorrow's citizen. Early help will pay immeasurable dividends.

And the reward for the teachers? Perhaps the following vignette conveys something of the experience. Writing of one scheme involving two tutors, Barbara Lancaster and Robin Powell, and a group of six children – four from Kosovo, one from Iraq and one from Kurdistan – Alison Wheatcroft recalled: 'On spotting their tutors, the children dropped everything and rushed to the ladies and covered them with hugs and kisses at the pure pleasure of seeing them. As a worldly person of some years, I had witnessed a sight that brought tears to my eyes.'

THE ESU NURSE WORK SHADOW PROGRAMME

In 1997 the ESU Nurse Work Shadow Programme came about via a casual conversation between ESU member Gill Prior and former ESU International Officer Ed Bracher whilst on an ESU visit to Bucharest. At the time Gill was a non-executive director for an NHS hospital in Bath and was involved with other hospitals in the area. Through her contacts, she was able to arrange a three to four week shadow programme for fully trained nurses. Over the following years the ESU Nurse Work Shadow Programme made it possible for nurses from countries as varied as Georgia, Brazil, Latvia, Lebanon, Poland and the Czech Republic to visit the UK and improve their English and their professional skills.

The applicants are of a high calibre. For instance Tereza Kolacna, from the Czech Republic, already held two degrees in surgery and spoke good English when she arrived in the UK. Her use of medical English impressed her fellow nurses. Commenting on her British visit, she said: 'I am grateful to the ESU for the opportunity to work with the wonderful people at the Great Western Hospital, Swindon and for all the hospitality I received.'

The programme has benefits for the nurses, the branches, the use of spoken English, and supporting hospitals such as the Great Western.

ESU INTERNSHIPS

The well-being of a society is greatly dependent upon the calibre of its politicians. For those interested in pursing a political career, becoming an intern is an excellent way of viewing the workings of government and opposition. In addition, becoming a political intern in a foreign country provides a fascinating contrast to Westminster. In our global village, it is essential that we learn from each other for the improvement of all of our political processes.

There are two ESU internships: the Capitol Hill Programme is based in Washington and the Assemblée Nationale Programme is based in Paris. Places are awarded on the basis of academic excellence and demonstrated active interest in areas such as politics, journalism and the Civil Service. For the Paris position, fluency in French is required.

The Paris internship programme is run in association with ESU France, which provides interns with placements, as well as support with finding accommodation. Previous interns have worked in the offices of Assemblée members such as M. Pierre Lellouche and M. Jacques Godfrain, and in the central office of the ruling party.

Official visa sponsorship and placements are provided for up to ten interns to work on Capitol Hill. In recent years ESU interns have worked in the offices of Vice-President Joe Biden and the late Senator Edward Kennedy. The social side of the programme affords an opportunity to develop relationships with British organisations, especially media organisations, based in Washington.

And the worth of these programmes?

> ... a valuable experience of living in France, a fascinating insight into French politics, an exciting role in the ever-shifting landscape of issues in one of Europe's most important countries ...
>
> It's a different system to Westminster ... almost like a democratic political religion, which you only get a sense of by spending time there. It's something you can't pick up from the books. It's 'The Hill' experience.

Today's interns are tomorrow's political leaders. It is to the benefit of all of us that they begin their international political experience at the earliest possible age and with the best mentors. An ESU internship is a cherished prize for the recipient and a valuable investment for the future of our society.

THE ESU'S DEBATING AND PUBLIC SPEAKING PROGRAMMES

Debating and public speaking are at the heart of what the ESU does. Being able to put your views across in a civilised and amicable manner is an indispensable skill for all of us. Moreover it is a skill which we could spend a lifetime acquiring and yet find room for improvement. The Centre for Speech and Debate coordinates the ESU's work in persuasive spoken English, and is the world leader in providing English language support for the use of debate and extended speech in an educational context. The Centre administers competitions such as the John Smith Memorial Mace, the Schools Mace, the Public Speaking Competition for Schools and the National Mooting Competition. Debating training is provided to teachers and students in the UK and abroad through a range of programmes, including Discover Your Voice, Debate Academy and the Speech and Debate Squad. The Centre has run the UK and US annual debate exchange since 1922 and selects and coaches the England Schools Debating team.

In 1954 *The Observer* newspaper was asked to establish a debating tournament for students at universities in the British Isles. Since then, generations of student debaters have sought to wield the Mace – the silver trophy awarded to the winning team. Those who have succeeded include several MPs, lawyers and eminent journalists. In 1994 the Lonrho company generously donated the Mace to the ESU which took over the administration of the tournament. Sadly that year also saw the death of Labour leader John Smith who, in 1962, had won the Mace for Glasgow University. In honour of his debating brilliance, put to such great effect as a lawyer and parliamentarian, the tournament was renamed The John Smith Memorial Mace.

One of many ESU debating success stories is a young man named Lewis Iwo. In 2002 Lewis took part in what was then known as the Tesco London Debate Programme, which has since developed into the London Debate Challenge, the ESU's largest ever education programme. His school, St Bonaventure's, a boys' comprehensive in East London, was one of the first to participate in the programme, which works with state-sector schools in London without a tradition of public debating. Lewis was talent-spotted by the student volunteers working with the ESU. He and his debating partner won the championship and were thrilled to visit Buckingham Palace to collect their awards from the Duke of Edinburgh. A year later, Lewis was the speaker in another team from St Bonaventure's who were named London Champions of the ESU's national public speaking competition. He went on to become the captain of the England Schools Debating Team which took part in the World Schools Debating championships. Lewis led his team to second place; he was individually named as the joint second best speaker of the championship. Together with his partner, Will Sharp, he went on to win the England final of the ESU Schools Mace: a fine clutch of trophies.

Inevitably one aspect of public speaking and debating competitions is coming in contact with your opponents – who may well have very different backgrounds and life experiences. Earlier we quoted a percipient comment which Prince Philip made regarding the 1991 World Schools Debating Championships in Edinburgh. It bears repetition: 'There are bound to be winners and losers in any contest, but I hope that all the competitors will go home with respect for their opponents and with the realisation that different opinions are no bar to lasting friendships.'

Undoubtedly many competitors have gone home with respect for their opponents – and lasting friendships have been made. The life of Sir Evelyn Wrench bears eloquent testament that different views and life experiences need be no barrier to friendship. In all walks of life, the better our views are expressed, the greater the chance that we may reach sound working agreements. The future of our planet depends upon sound working agreements from many people of different cultures, continents and life experiences.

In 2002 the ESU took a high profile in a special debate held in the House of Commons, a Nuffield Enquiry chaired by Sir Trevor McDonald, the broadcaster and ESU Governor. Sir Len Appleyard, husband of Lady Appleyard (she was then ESU Deputy Chairman and Chairman of the Education Committee), was closely involved. Speaking in the House of Lords debate were the then ESU Chairman Lord Watson, Baroness Hooper, a former ESU Governor, and Lord Quirk, a former Governor and Vice-Chairman of the English Language Council. And the subject of the debate? The importance of British people learning foreign languages. There is a pleasing symmetry in

ESU Governors not only advocating English as a global language but also emphasising the relevance of British people learning other peoples' languages. And there is another pleasing symmetry in ESU Governors demonstrating that debating and public speaking are for all of us.

7
The Alumnus Experience

'ESU scholarships really do change lives!' (William Glover)

We have seen how, as a young man, Sir Evelyn Wrench was enchanted by the hospitality so freely shown him in America and Canada. From personal experience, he realised the wisdom of the old adage 'Travel broadens the mind'. He also realised that to understand another culture one must interact with it. Too often we travel as tourists, gliding past cultures that we don't begin to understand. Wrench knew that if you have a reason for being in a country and interacting with its inhabitants then you have a marked advantage. Furthermore if you meet people not only in their workplaces but also in their homes, you connect with them in a manner which goes far beyond mere tourism. To this end, the ESU began scholarships in the 1920s. Only the dangers of the Second World War stopped the two-way flow of ESU scholars between Britain and the USA. After the war Lillian Moore and Yvonne Theobald developed unrivalled expertise in administering a huge network of sponsors, scholars and scholarships. Indeed some scholars later became sponsors. At a formative time in their lives, they had received a chance to interact with other cultures and thereby develop. With a keen sense of gratitude, some were freely prepared to pay back.

Today, in 2010, the ESU has accumulated over eighty years of administering all manner of scholarships. Each scholarship recipient automatically becomes an ESU alumnus and thereby privy to a well-established infrastructure of ongoing support and activities.

For tens of thousands of ESU scholars, 'the alumnus experience' has been a never-to-be-forgotten episode in their lives, a springboard to greater confidence and enhanced personal, social and professional development. Many ESU alumni are 'multipliers', i.e. people who have considerable influence with others. Typical examples are professional people and businesspeople. Perhaps the archetypal example of a multiplier is a teacher, whether in the classroom or out of it. In the course of a professional life, a poor teacher can turn hundreds, perhaps even thousands of people, off a subject. Conversely a good teacher can turn hundreds, perhaps thousands of people, on to a subject. Even more importantly, a good teacher turns people on to the most important subjects of all: their own personal, social and professional development. When former pupils become teachers themselves (again, whether in the classroom or out of it), the good becomes multiplied. With each succeeding generation, the benefits continue to accumulate.

Consequently investing in 'multipliers' is one of the best investments that any society can possibly make. The ripples spread; and who knows where they end? To convey a sense of the life-changing impact of the alumnus experience, we have asked a few of the many thousands of ESU alumni to describe their own encounters in their own words. This is what they have to say.

JOURNEY OF A LIFETIME

Brian Marsh OBE
President, The ESU Alumni

It was in 1936, nearly seventy-five years ago, that Noel Gee, David Carling and others founded with great enthusiasm what was then called the 'British Alumni Club', even as the dark clouds of the Second World War were beginning to gather.

The Club was open to British boys who had studied in the USA under the ESU Secondary School Exchange programme and, within twenty years, it had shifted its name away from the 'British Alumni Club' to the 'British American Alumni'. Few of us can escape the political fashions of the day and the concept of 'clubbishness' in the years after the Second World War began to seem too exclusive. The new name also reflected the fact that the Alumni was open to American members, although in reality it remained a British association.

The B.A.A. had its own President (Douglas Fairbanks Jnr) and its own Chairman and Honorary Officers. It had its own cuff-links and neckties and even its own magazine, called *The Griffin*. The B.A.A. most especially welcomed the arrival of female alumnae into its midst – they made the social gatherings so much more decorative and, indeed, amusing. Fortunately the organisation survived in this separate form for about forty years, after which it was renamed the ESU Alumni and subsumed into the parent organisation at Dartmouth House.

As we know from our history books and from personal experience, most forms of progress have a tendency to bring losses in their wake. In the case of the British Alumni Club and its successor organisations, the progress which has done the most damage is, without doubt, the remorseless advance of air travel. Up to and including the 1960s, the twenty-five or so departing students would sail to New York from Southampton, a journey of five days, during which lifelong friendships were forged, giving the B.A.A. a real and lasting link to its membership as the students returned to the UK and went their various ways.

Since the transatlantic sea crossings were terminated and replaced by air flights to different destinations, these excited teenage sea-borne friendships have vanished and with them has gone one of the great joys of winning the scholarship. The Alumni Association has survived however: it presides over several reunions of its members each year and publishes a periodical newsletter. It raises money when it can for the ESU Educational funds.

The Alumni's seventy-fifth birthday (2011) will no doubt be duly marked and celebrated. However it is interesting to reflect that, with the advent of all the recent and growing environmental opposition to air travel (which would not have been anticipated fifty years ago), the time might yet come when twenty-five or so ESU scholars will once again, as an increasingly cohesive social unit, mount the steps to a transatlantic liner and embark upon the journey of a lifetime.

MY GAP YEAR IN AMERICA: TABOR ACADEMY, MASSACHUSETTS, 2005/6

Thomas Wordley, Student

I have just had the best year of my life at Tabor Academy, in the small town of Marion in Massachusetts. There was nothing about it I would alter, apart from making it longer. In only one year, so much can change. Your perceptions of who you are and what you can achieve can become radically different. I'm amazed at how much I've changed for the better. I could never have imagined that I would benefit so much from this gap year.

Academically my experience has made me realise where I want to be in the future and that I can achieve whatever I want in life by working hard for it. My teachers at Tabor were very friendly and deeply caring. They genuinely want to see you do well at school and are always understanding and ready to offer help. Their teaching methods are designed to instil confidence. As the year went by and my confidence increased, so too did my grades. I was thrilled to achieve an 88 grade point average, with a score of 4 out of 5 in my AP Biology test. I worked hard and achieved my goals.

Socially I am amazed at the many close friends I have made and with whom I feel I will always keep in touch. In fact I am already planning on going back to America next summer to see them.

At first it was hard to interact with groups of friends which had already existed for years. In reality, this difficulty is merely a mental barrier; nevertheless it's a barrier which you have to break through as quickly as possible. After that, the hardest thing is remembering everyone's names. People at Tabor couldn't have been more friendly and welcoming; this really helped me to settle in at school.

Sport provided an avenue for friendship and, although I had to battle with constant tendonitis in both ankles, I enjoyed every painful minute of it. A really good way of forging a stronger bond with someone is by staying at their home on open weekends or holidays. You get to know them in a much more relaxed environment and you have a chance to meet the family behind the friend. With my friend Eric Franks, or, to me, EJ, I had the pleasure of staying at his house on many occasions. His family couldn't have been nicer to me and I had a great time at their house. They treated me as their son; in fact, that's what Lisa (EJ's mum) used to call me. I really miss them and can't wait to see them again, next year.

America is culturally quite different from England. Generally people are much more confident. Certainly at Tabor sport is very important. It's a way of enjoying yourself, whilst keeping fit and learning key skills, such as leadership.

When you stay at peoples' houses on open weekends or on school holidays, you really begin to engage with the culture. Most meals are held as a family around the dining table, which is something I really enjoyed and feel that many young people today are missing out on. At first, you're very conscious of the need to be polite and well-behaved – which, of course, stops you being at your ease. Soon, however, you start to relax and everything seems to come naturally. There's a sense of integration. When you first feel that sense of integration you realise that you're fully embracing the gap-year experience.

If you want to enjoy your year as much as I did, the key thing is to have an open mind and look for the good in everything. People will joke about your accent pretty much all the time but that's simply because they're fascinated by it – although I'm still not quite sure why. As a whole, people are really welcoming. They genuinely want to get to know you and, inevitably, strong friendships develop. My gap-year experience has changed my entire perception of what I can do and where I want to go in life. I'd been told that it would benefit me and, up to a point, I believed this – but I never would have guessed that the benefit would have been so tremendous. THANK YOU!!

I would like to add that writing this essay was one of the hardest things I've ever done. This was because I felt that the act of writing it was putting an end to a chapter of my life that I didn't really want to close. But, after my year at Tabor Academy, thankfully I know who I am and where I'm going.

THE GERTRUDE COLE SCHOLARSHIP

Mark Featherstone-Witty
Founding Principal/CEO of The Liverpool Institute for Performing Arts
(co-founded with Sir Paul McCartney)
Recipient of the Gertrude Cole (Postgraduate) Scholarship, 1974

When I was awarded the Gertrude Cole Scholarship (administered by the ESU), my parents were convinced that I was the only person who had applied. They were appalled that their 27-year-old son, who seemed to be putting off growing up for as long as possible, had found yet another ruse to delay getting a proper job. I had planned to teach, but teaching-practice in Gateshead had severely dented my confidence.

The ESU's Lillian Moore managed the selection process. For some reason, I had feared that she might be arrogant or pompous. Of course my fears were totally unfounded and Lillian and I became firm friends until her sadly early death.

I had been given a year in a liberal arts college in Winter Park – a retirement town, north of Orlando, in Florida. Winter Park was dotted with lakes. I had an apartment, on campus, near one of them. How lucky can you get?

My luck continued. My supervisor took a shine to me so, despite college bureaucracy, he was determined to ensure I took a Master of Education degree that was not simply tailored to the qualification, but was also an experience of what the college was best at doing. So I attended lectures that had nothing overtly to do with my course of study, but which were nevertheless exciting and informative.

A lifelong interest was acting, so I hurried along to the theatre department and eagerly applied to appear in anything suitable, as well as taking courses outside the assigned curriculum. This initiative led to appearing in 'a major motion picture' (aren't they all?) as a featured actor, playing a gay hairdresser, Nigel of London.

The audition took place in an office block, just off a busy highway. The scene asked me to comfort a girl who had just been molested – a somewhat demanding request to come, out of the blue, at 10.30 am, but then that's all part of being an actor.

I was amazed to find recently that I could buy a copy of the film from Amazon. This isn't to say it was any good! My delightful film teacher (another course I took outside the assigned curriculum) advised me that, if the film ever came to Europe, I should think twice about getting involved in any publicity.

Naturally my parents were even more appalled; this was not at all the proper job they had in mind. (However this didn't seem to put them off visiting me and enjoying a spell in the glorious Florida sunshine …)

Years afterwards, I was dating a teacher whom I encouraged to apply for the Gertrude Cole Scholarship. She too managed to gain it. She later became my wife. So the ESU played a formative role for both of us.

Aside from gaining the only scholarship in my life, what lasting effect did that year (aside from another degree) have on me? I remember the vitality of the teaching (very different indeed from my first UK degree), the heavenly weather, hitting an intellectual stride, and finding friends for life (as well as some gorgeous temporary girlfriends who just loved the English accent). I was ripe for experience – and the USA gave me an experience which has never left me.

QUENTIN LETTS, POLITICAL JOURNALIST AND COLUMNIST

Recipient of an Undergraduate Scholarship
(Bellarmine College, Kentucky, 1980–81)

Even at 10 pm the air in Kentucky was hot and humid. It was late August 1980 and my school-friend Chris Payton and I had just landed in Louisville at the end of a long journey from London. I was seventeen, Chris was eighteen. Both of us were ludicrously overdressed in thick tweed jackets, slacks, English shoes and ties. All I knew about the American climate was that it seemed to rain a lot – or at least it did in episodes of *Kojak* when Telly Savalas was frequently drenched by New York downpours. No one had mentioned the heat; on arrival in Louisville, it almost knocked us out.

Courtesy of the ESU, we had arrived at Bellarmine College, all fees paid for four years if we so wanted. As it happens, both of us stayed for just one year – but what a fantastic year it was, not only a huge culture shock but also educational in the broadest sense. We learned to drink bourbon, drive big cars, play softball, stay on the right side of Kentucky maidens' fathers and pronounce our host city's name the Kentucky way – 'Louavull'.

That year I did a lot of growing up. Looking back, I realise that I behaved like an impertinent ingrate to the college authorities. I wrote thunderous criticisms of the Dean in the college newspaper. Appalled by the idea of 8 am classes, I dropped out of Statistics. I complained about the provincialism of the local media and kept droning on about the desirability of national healthcare. But I had a complete blast during my time in Kentucky and am incredibly grateful that Bellarmine's authorities didn't pack me home on the first available plane, as they must have been sorely tempted.

I had arrived with the vaguely left-wing leanings of a typical European teenager. Such views were soon challenged! Bellarmine, a Roman Catholic college, had firm ideas about morality and there were strict visiting hours if we wished to stray to the women's accommodation block. Consequently corridor-creeping attained the status of an art form. As kegs of beer weren't allowed indoors, we held parties in a friend's downstairs room, placing a keg outside the window, with a long hose attached. The Dean, who clearly was not as bad a stick as I'd originally thought, praised our ingenuity and suggested that we might make good lawyers.

1980 was the year of the Carter-Reagan election. From what I had read about Ronald Reagan in the British newspapers before travelling, the man was obviously a no-hoper. A few days in Louisville put me right. The United States was in despair over the Iran hostages' affair. We tied yellow ribbons to the trees and painted a vast Stars and Stripes on the college lawns to show Ayatollah Khomeini our outrage. President Carter was viewed as a weak leader who had failed to stand up to a hostile Tehran.

Reagan's message of smaller, stronger government found ready believers among our fellow students – not least perhaps because they were holding down part-time jobs in order to pay their college fees. Chris and I had arrived from a Britain where generous grants were still provided for university education. Such independence, such self-sufficiency by students, was a revelation to us. That year in Kentucky cured me of my naïve belief in socialism!

Chris and I were regularly paraded like performing monkeys, being asked to 'say something in an English accent'. Hardly surprising, perhaps ... Some of our friends had never been outside Kentucky, let alone the United States. We could not have been made more welcome. We were issued with repeated invitations to friends' homes and spent a memorable Thanksgiving with the Reed family in Shawneeville, Ohio, singing 'Frosty the Snowman' for the first time and piling into a Volkswagen Beetle to go bowling. The local newspaper sent along a reporter and photographer to interview us, as though we had landed from Mars.

We used to visit the house of a friend whose single mother lived near Fort Knox, Kentucky, in a small settlement notable only for its railway level crossing. The vast trains would go loping by, bells clanging dolefully ... a scene straight out of Tennessee Williams.

Naturally we motored down to Florida for spring-break. I shared the driving with Stuart Rooney, another ESU scholar, who had a car. Spring-break was a week of beach parties and bikini competitions sponsored by Camel cigarettes. I remember a feeling of nascent adulthood, of freedom, of material plenty under a broad sky.

Stuart played rugby for Louisville (they had a good team) and I was given a few games in one of the lower-level teams. I was hopeless at baseball but used to watch the Bellarmine basketball team. Two of the lads were on our corridor of the dorms. They were about 6′ 8″ and ate three times as much as other mortals.

Shortly after becoming president, Ronald Reagan was shot. We were glued to the news all day. Fortunately he survived. John Lennon was less lucky. The night he died, girls ran along our dorm corridors, screaming in shock. The radio stations played non-stop Beatles music for weeks. It made a change from the more usual diet of Christopher Cross and Willie Nelson.

Although lost to time and distance, the friendships I made that year were some of the most vivid I have known: sardonic Jim, from Chicago, who was only nineteen but had the world-weariness of a man of forty; toothy Denis, from Kentucky, who remained amazingly stoical despite the death of his father; a hippie called Kevin Castor ('KC') who called everyone 'man', even if they were female; a beautiful basketball player called Gina; a Zuleika Dobson from Washington called Cynthia; and Chris's crazy girlfriend Erica, who revised for her literature exams while working as a checkout girl at the local Walmart.

Thank you, ESU, for the year of a lifetime and for showing me that the American way of life is not just about spending and the liberal coasts but is also about hard work, hard-earned merit and that severe but loyal land they call the Mid-West.

MEMORIES OF A SUMMER AT THE BANFF SCHOOL OF FINE ARTS

Tasmin Little, Internationally Acclaimed Violinist

I remember my first meeting with Belinda Norman-Butler when I was still a pupil at the Yehudi Menuhin School and just seventeen years old. She came up to me after a performance that I had given at the end-of-year concerts and spoke to me about the English-Speaking Union's scholarship programme, suggesting that, at some stage in the future, I might consider applying for a grant to study at one of the summer schools.

Her words stayed with me as I continued my studies. In 1984, during my second year at the Guildhall School of Music, I decided that I wished to apply, as I hoped to spend the following summer at the Banff School of Fine Arts in Canada. I had heard about the summer courses there and, in particular, about a violin teacher called Mr Fenyves, who had a tremendous reputation. I decided to try for the Banff Scholarship and I remember my audition well – Belinda was there with Edward

The Queen Mother's 1941 visit to Dartmouth House. Dame Edith Lyttelton on the right. (Copyright Press Association)

T. S. Eliot flanked by Alicia Street (left) and Beatrice Warde (right) at a Books Across the Sea (BAS) meeting in 1944

Winston Churchill and Dwight D. Eisenhower (Topical Press Agency Ltd)

A 1963 exchange visit between Bristol and Kentucky branches of the ESU. Eric Dehn is on the extreme right.

Belinda Norman-Butler receives the ESU Churchill Medal from Baroness Brigstocke

A celebrated trio of ESU musical alumni: Robert Cohen, Tasmin Little and Stephen Isserlis (courtesy Aldo Carbonari)

Baroness Soames

Lillian Moore

John Bond, ESU scholar at Cate School
(courtesy Cate School/Sir John Bond)

Lewis Iwo, ESU debating star

ESU Headquarters, Dartmouth House

Two delighted students receive their debating awards from ESU President HRH The Duke of Edinburgh (kind permission Buckingham Palace)

The ESU 85th Anniversary celebrations at Westminster Abbey (courtesy David Cavill – event photography)

ESU alumnus and Chinese Ambassador, Madame Fu Ying, delivers the ESU Churchill lecture

The 2006 International Conference at Marlborough House (courtesy David Cavill – event photography)

HRH The Duke of Edinburgh (kind permission Buckingham Palace)

Greenfield, the eminent music critic, and another member of the adjudicating panel. I played the first movement of the Brahms violin concerto and then spoke to the panel about my hopes of studying with Mr Fenyves in Banff the following summer. When I was asked if any of the other summer schools were of interest to me, I remember my total honesty (which in retrospect seems quite precocious and certainly risky!) in saying that I was only interested in the Banff scholarship. When I received the news that I had been successful in my application for Banff, I was immensely excited and couldn't wait to go. The scholarship was most generous; it covered my flight, tuition, food and board for the duration of the course – expenses that I simply could not have afforded without the help of the English-Speaking Union.

That summer in Banff altered the course of my life. I knew at once that Mr Fenyves was the violin teacher with whom I wanted to continue my studies. Up until that point, I had no idea where I would go after finishing my degree at the Guildhall School of Music and this was something that had worried me greatly. In addition, the School of Fine Arts was an immersion into many different artistic disciplines. I loved being surrounded by writers, dancers, jazz musicians and painters, all in the same magnificent complex. The Banff summer school is situated in an inspiring and dramatic setting and the six weeks that I spent there soon flew past. I attended as many of Mr Fenyves's open classes as I could, as well as hearing masterclasses given by famous 'cellists and pianists. I practised in the special huts in the woods that surround the campus; it is quite something to practise whilst watching a vast array of wildlife, as Banff is a National Park and the animals are free to roam anywhere. We were even warned about the bears! One day I was sitting on the grass when a big, graceful deer sauntered past. The whole experience was so very different. It inspired me to work as hard as I could to maximise every opportunity that the summer school was giving me.

When I returned to London, I took a bold decision not to continue at the Guildhall for the full four years and decided to make the coming third year my final one there, so that I could continue my tuition with Mr Fenyves during the following winter in Toronto. I worked hard to make that dream a reality, but I would not have had the courage or determination to do so without the opportunity that had been given to me to go to Banff. For that I am indebted to the English-Speaking Union's music scholarship programme.

I have retained my links with the English-Speaking Union and have given many concert performances to raise money for the music scholarships. As my experience attests, these scholarships are vital opportunities which can be life-changing for anyone fortunate enough to receive one.

SIR JOHN BOND, SECONDARY SCHOOL EXCHANGE SCHOLAR 1959

Former Group Chairman of HSBC Holdings PLC
Former Chairman of HSBC Bank PLC
Chairman of Vodafone Group PLC

Aided by wartime evacuation in 1941, my mother ensured that I was born in Oxford, in the hope that one day I would attend the university. However in 1958 I failed the entrance exam. When my headmaster mentioned ESU Exchange Scholarships, they seemed a pretty good idea. The alternative was a rather frosty reception at home. September 1959 found me in Cate School, near Santa Barbara, in California.

During my childhood I had only left England twice, once for a week in Holland and then for a few weeks with a family in France, learning the language. America took my breath away: the space, the confidence, the energy, the 'can-do' attitude. I had never seen an avocado in my life, yet here they were in the school salads!

I was taught superbly in a thought-provoking manner. I learned American history and literature. I took part in inter-school debates; I wrote poetry for the school magazine; I played baseball; I surfed; I hiked canyons; I lived with American families during the holidays. I learned that there were different forms of democracy and of government.

Living in another country not only teaches you about its culture and history; it also gives you an objective, comparative view of your own country. So I gained a new perspective on the United Kingdom.

Inspired by my ESU experience, at the end of a fabulous year in California, I decided to explore the world. I sailed as a deck-hand from Long Beach, via Hawaii, Japan and the Philippines, before being discharged in Hong Kong. There I got a job as a disc-jockey on a troopship sailing to the UK, via Singapore, Colombo and Aden.

Asia, with its different cultures and wonderful people, fascinated me.

By the time I reached the UK, I knew that I was going to return to Asia to work, ideally for an organisation that had business interests in the USA. I was fortunate enough to find HSBC.

I joined HSBC in 1961 and left the UK at the age of twenty-two. I spent the next thirty years working in Hong Kong, Thailand, Indonesia and USA. It is no exaggeration to say that the ESU changed my life.

Without my ESU-sponsored experience, I would not understand the world's most powerful nation; I might never have experienced the amazing terrain it has to offer: mountains, forests, deserts, rivers, oceans. I would not have sent my daughter to university there; I would not own a home in America or sit on the board of an American company. I would not be able to enjoy baseball, ice hockey and American football.

As we know, the ESU was founded by Sir Evelyn Wrench in 1918 to promote 'international understanding and friendship through the use of the English language'. Today we would call this a mission statement. It embraces both a noble cause – international understanding – and a practical means of achieving it, through a common language.

At present I am an Adviser to Tsinghua University's Business School in Beijing. Our Honorary President is Zhu Rhongji, the former Premier of China. In 2005 I listened to him instructing the Dean of the Business School to conduct at least 50% of the courses in English within two years. Today 60% of all classes are taught in English. Conversely I'm very pleased to note that my old school in England now teaches Mandarin.

Currently I sit on the boards of A.P Moller-Maersk in Copenhagen and Shui On Land in Hong Kong. Although my fellow directors are Danish and Chinese respectively, both boards conduct business in English.

With great foresight, the ESU has opened an office in China. Exchange programmes between British and Chinese high schools would be a great way to promote understanding with a rising power, in the same way that the ESU did for me, over fifty years ago.

'FROM BIBLES TO BICYCLES': THE HISTORY OF THE BELL TOWER SCHOLARSHIP

William Glover, Chautauqua Bell Tower Scholarship, 1998

It is impossible to describe the sense of serenity which envelops you as you enter the hallowed grounds of the Chautauqua Institution in New York. This is the America of Mark Twain: white picket fences and pretty clapboard cottages, the red brick path and Bestor Plaza, the yachts on the lake and the musicians in their shacks. Dance, drama, art, literature and leisure; all, any, some or none of these pursuits are yours to explore. A word too often used to describe Chautauqua is 'unique' and yet that is precisely what the institution is. Chautauqua is an experience individual to each Chautauquan.

From that very first Sunday school teachers' camp in 1876, Chautauqua has offered the chance for each and every voice to sing its song, to explore the symphony of your life and to travel at a rhythm divorced from the constraints of the humdrum 'real world'. Here at Chautauqua the scholar takes flight, discovering a personal history unknown just months before, when applicants face the daunting ordeal of being interviewed at Dartmouth House.

For me personally, every line of prose written as I explored Chautauqua in all its guises inscribed an indelible link with the institution and the ESU on my soul. There has been an unending succession of experiences. Each encounter has built the pieces that make me whole. Chautauqua has become part of me, in the way that it becomes part of every scholar, every Chautauquan.

Through the highs and lows of the life that have followed those first tentative steps 'on the grounds', Chautauqua and its people have been core to my experience. When I became a part of Chautauqua, I discovered a hitherto unimagined *family*. Not a year has passed since 1998 that I have not made frequent visits *home* to Western New York. Within my new-found family, the richest relationship has been the one which I have with Professor H. R and Mrs Carol McCarthy Duhme (Carol and Dick, to us scholars).

Immediately upon my return to England, I started to trace the history of my scholarship. Many and varied were the tales I had to tell in order to circumvent the regulations involved in tracking down the myriad of young scholars who, over the subsequent years, had spread worldwide. My favourite tale is one of tracing a scholar from the early 1960s, now an eminent professor in Canada; this involved my pretence of being a long-lost cousin.

I unearthed clergy, knights of the realm, journalists, academics and headmasters amongst the group. However the most romantic tale involved two scholars who met for the first time on the Chautauqua trail to discover that it was also a path to love and marriage.

In February 1999 I hosted a party at Dartmouth House honouring

Carol and Dick. Old friends were re-united and it was on this visit that I took Dick to see his grandmother's ancestral home in Scotland for the first time in his eighty-five years.

This scholarship, which has meant so much to so many, was conceived during a fireside chat in the early 1930s, at the home of Institution President Arthur Bestor and his lifelong friend President Franklin D. Roosevelt. There began the history of British academics embracing the Chautauqua Season. I have been fortunate enough to become acquainted with industry, religious, political and world leaders, as well as cleaners, cooks and maids at Chautauqua. In researching the history of the scholarship I found no greater witness than President Bestor's daughter Mary Frances, a woman who knew Henry Ford and Thomas Edison as uncles and Presidents and Prime Ministers as friends.

My own scholarship elevated me to a senior pastoral post at Chautauqua, to a position on the teaching faculty, and catapulted me into the shoes of Eleanor Roosevelt as I addressed the topic of 'Education in the New Millennium' from the same platform that gave the world FDR's 'I Hate War' speech and Eleanor's motherly words of wisdom. It was at Chautauqua that I cut my first CD. It was because of Chautauqua that I addressed student groups following 9/11, at both Ground Zero and The Pentagon. It was because of Chautauqua that I toured China's schools in 2004, and it was because of this scholarship that I came to ESU Eastbourne, developed an international education project with Glasgow University, established a charity book company, established a globally significant gap-year support project for students, and became Author-in-Residence to ESU Eastbourne.

Will Glover was Bell Tower and Rebecca Richmond Scholar to the Chautauqua Institution, New York in 1998. As a result of his scholarship, he returned to Chautauqua as the Director of Youth Ministry in the Department of Religion for the Institution's 'Season of Renewal' in 1999. His work with the Revd Dr Ross Mackenzie continued for a further two years and he served Chautauqua as a consultant and strategic planner in religious programming. Will also taught in the Special Studies Faculty at Chautauqua and was invited as a main platform speaker to address the Institution on the topic of Education in 2000. In 1999 he was awarded the Washington University Medallion in Fine Arts by Professor H. R. Duhme (Bell Tower Scholarship benefactor) for his research on the Duhme School of Sculpture.

As a result of his experiences at Chautauqua, Will served for ten years as a consultant to the Speech/Language Pathology Unit at Randolph Academy, NY; he became a writer in the English Department at Western Kentucky University and he completed a Masters Degree in Literacy and Professional Development based around a class taken as scholar at Chautauqua.

As a result of his Bell Tower scholarship, Will joined ESU Eastbourne, where he currently serves as Youth President and Author-in-Residence. In 2006, in conjunction with Glasgow University and the ESU, Will led an international education project based around the role of English in stimulating environmental concern.

As an alumnus, Will has encouraged a number of his students to undertake Capitol Hill, SSE and associated ESU scholarships. Since 2004 he has served on the Professional-Scholarships Committee at Dartmouth House, annually selecting both the Bell Tower and Walter Hines Page Scholars. ESU scholarships really do change lives!

ALISON MARSHMAN, PROMINENT EDUCATIONALIST

Specialist in Special Education Needs
Walter Hines Page Scholarship, 1995

'It could well be that, if some of the time and energy spent in esoteric pedagogical research were devoted to examining critically some of the best ways which other countries have adopted of tackling problems which we have in common, much good to our children would come out of it.
(Clegg and Megson, 1973)

In October 1995, approaching my forty-ninth birthday, it was with a mixture of incredulity and excitement that I arrived in Austin, Texas. I was teacher-in-charge of a unit, based in a primary school, for children with speech, language and learning needs. The Page scholarship provided an opportunity to examine provision in the USA for children with similar special educational needs (SEN). With the invaluable support of the team at Dartmouth House and the generosity and hospitality of members of the English-Speaking Union in the USA, a hectic but inspiring three-week programme had been devised, including staying in six locations in five states and visiting ten schools and four universities. On return to the UK, I compiled a report and was invited to describe my findings at schools, universities and other local, county and national organisations. The entire experience helped to shape my professional life.

Observations and interviews conducted throughout my stay revealed similarities between our two countries, some of which were immediately apparent. Many pupils had difficulties similar to those of the children with whom I worked and some were in mainstream classes alongside their typically-developing peers. I encountered teachers striving to meet needs in under-resourced schools, a familiar scenario to me. However, as I became more familiar with the American education system, interesting differences were revealed.

American speech and language therapists, known as 'pathologists', were jointly qualified as licensed pathologists and certified teachers and there was at least one in every school in the public (state) system. Speech and language therapy was an educational service. Pathologists were full members of the school's faculty, salaried from the school budget. UK therapists were most likely to be found in a language unit, funded through Health Trusts; a fundamental difference between provision in the two countries. Advice for teachers and support for children was readily available in the USA. This was not so in the vast majority of schools in the UK.

In schools, responses to the question: 'Is there a named person with responsibility for special educational needs?' revealed a common theme of shared responsibility. The words 'team' and 'committee' occurred frequently and there was no evidence of a single class teacher having responsibility for SEN throughout the school as was often the case in the UK.

Parental involvement in the education of children with special needs was regarded as an area of great importance. Repeated reference was made to legal requirements: 'Annual Reviews'; 'Individual Education Plans'; 'Parent/Teacher Conferences'. However, one professional expressed an opinion that levels of communication varied 'tremendously'. The importance of parent/teacher communication was stressed in student training but constraints of time and parental availability and willingness to attend conferences could lead to a difference between theory and practice. In the mid-1990s 'parent power' seemed an important factor in the USA; however it was less easy to discover just how widespread and how effective it was.

The term 'integration' was not used in the USA to describe provision in which pupils with SEN receive all or part of their education in mainstream classrooms. The most commonly used term was 'inclusion', indicating that pupils, whatever their disability, should attend the neighbourhood school. However some of the interviewees expressed doubt as to whether this was appropriate in all cases. On two separate occasions I observed children being removed from the classroom as their presence was felt to be too disruptive. This was distressing for all concerned, adding weight to the doubts expressed during the interviews. Shortly after my visit, I was to see evidence of similar concerns in the UK.

I was impressed by the dedication of the professionals and the willingness of teachers, pathologists and students to share their time, knowledge and experience. Many of the issues being addressed at that time in the USA were later found to be significant in the UK as, through legislation, efforts were made to move towards a fairer and more inclusive educational system.

An additional benefit derived from my visit was a heightened awareness of the skills required to be an effective classroom observer, which had an immediate effect on my practice both as a teacher and as a researcher. Ten years later, thanks to the Teaching Awards Trust, I visited Nairobi to study SEN provision in Kenya. The expertise acquired through my Page Scholarship helped me to make the most of the opportunities presented.

In conclusion, a note of caution. The UK and the USA have been described as two countries separated by a common language. I managed to throw a school in Buffalo into confusion by announcing that I'd 'lost my mac'. Members of faculty were promptly dispatched all over the school to search for a computer. Somewhat embarrassingly, all I'd mislaid was my raincoat!

THE GREATEST ADVENTURE OF MY LIFE

The Rt. Hon. Michael Howard, QC, MP

In 1963, thanks to the English-Speaking Union, I set off on the greatest adventure of my life. Together with John Toulmin, now a distinguished judge, I had been selected to represent the Cambridge Union on a debating tour of the United States. We had just eight weeks to debate at 540 universities and colleges west of the Mississippi. It was an exhausting schedule but we loved every minute of it.

Our very first debate wasn't in the US at all, but at McGill University in Montreal. We spent a rather tense weekend at a time of great discord between the French- and English-speaking people of that part of Canada. From Montreal we flew to New York for a briefing, before starting the debating tour proper at Eau Claire, Wisconsin. Debating was part of the syllabus at many American universities. This briefing was our first experience of debate coaches and the rigorous and rather stylised approach which they brought to the subject.

From Wisconsin we made our way through the Mid-West, taking in Iowa, Nebraska, the Dakotas and Missouri. Almost fifty years later, so many vignettes remain fresh in my mind.

By bus, we crossed into South Dakota, with the Great Plains of the Mid-West stretching out in all directions, flat and featureless, as far as the eye could see. The sign that greeted us as we crossed the State line read, 'Welcome to South Dakota, land of infinite variety'.

In Missouri our itinerary included a visit to Independence and the Harry Truman Library. We were privileged to have an audience with the great man himself, an unforgettable encounter.

On 22 November 1963 we were in Moscow, Idaho, checking out of our hotel, when I saw a crowd of people gathered around a television set in the corner of the lobby. Someone said, 'The President's been shot!' I assumed they were talking about the ruler of some South American state. Then the full horror of the assassination became apparent.

It was an extraordinary time to be in the United States. During the following days, the outpouring of grief which followed the President's death seemed to drown out everything else. Our debates in Pullman, Washington, Portland, Oregon and San Francisco were cancelled. However the football match between the University of California at Berkeley and Stratford University went ahead. Our hosts were kind enough to take us to see it.

It was not until we arrived in Los Angeles that the mood lightened. In LA, our debating schedule resumed at Occidental College, an *alma mater* of President Obama's. We were entertained by the college debating coach, who rejoiced in the name of Lee Roloff. Lee took us to a striptease show in Hollywood. At one juncture he chortled, 'I hope you enjoy the next act – she's the wife of our philosophy professor!'

Subsequently we went to Dallas, just three weeks after the assassination. We were shown the building from which Lee Harvey Oswald fired the fatal shot and the grassy knoll which the President's motorcade had reached when he was hit. In Dallas, at that time, the mood was markedly different from the rest of the country. The general attitude was, 'It may have happened in Dallas – but don't think it's anything to do with us. We're not responsible ...'

Our debating tour ended, just before Christmas, with a debate at Louisiana State University at Baton Rouge, followed by a memorable twenty-four hours in New Orleans. I stayed on in the United States for another seven months, working for a law firm in New York and making friendships which have lasted all my life.

I have no doubt that this American visit was one of the seminal experiences of my life, leaving me with a deep and lasting affection for the United States and its people. I shall always be grateful to the English-Speaking Union for making it possible. I owe it a great debt.

8
ESU Branches

'The membership is the bedrock of the English-Speaking Union.'
(Valerie Mitchell)

The ESU is, of course, a charity. But, within its remit of charitable activities, is it a membership organisation or an educational organisation? The answer, of course, is that it is both membership organisation *and* educational organisation. By balancing membership and educational benefits, the ESU achieves a rare symbiosis. An ESU branch member, enjoying a social outing, with convivial and like-minded spirits, knows that there is a vital educational purpose to everything which the ESU does. Such knowledge imbues the event with extra significance.

At present, there are nearly forty ESU branches across England and Wales, with more than 5,500 members. Each branch actively supports the aims of the ESU and organises its activities to meet the needs of local and visiting members. Typical programmes include concerts, talks, literary evenings and outings to places of interest. These events enable members to raise funds, which may be used for local sponsorship, exchange visits or centrally organised ESU programmes.

How does one come to join a branch of the ESU? In his memoirs, Sir Hugh Jones, an ESU Director-General in the 1970s, recounts an amusing anecdote of how Denis Rattle, father of the famous conductor, joined. One evening Rattle Senior set off to attend a meeting at a local community centre. Such centres are often rabbit warrens of deserted corridors, characteristically devoid of directions. On the night in question, this proved the case. In his futile search, Rattle chanced on 'a couple of lonesome people in an empty room who told him they were trying to form a branch of an organisation called the English-Speaking Union.' From such an inauspicious beginning, Denis Rattle created the Liverpool branch and made it the biggest in the UK, with a commensurate amount of US/UK exchanges. In Hugh Jones's trenchant words, Rattle's family 'lived, ate and slept the ESU'.

Interestingly, Liverpool and Merseyside branch of the ESU now hold their meetings in the library of the Athenaeum; no, not the Athenaeum in London, but the one in Liverpool. This was founded in 1797, preceding the establishment of the London club, to provide a meeting place where ideas and information could be exchanged in pleasant surroundings. Its library, one of the greatest proprietary libraries in the world, now hosts the Liverpool and Merseyside Public Speaking Competition branch final. In 1848 Washington Irving, in his sketch book, wrote, 'One of the first places to which a stranger is taken in Liverpool is the Athenaeum, the greatest literary resort of the place.' An amenable environment for conducting ESU business ... One wonders whether, if Denis Rattle had found the meeting he was looking for all those years ago (or simply wandered into another room), what might – or might not – have transpired. Perhaps it's better to celebrate what has happened: a proud ESU branch well established in Washington Irving's 'greatest literary resort'.

As the ESU was originally formed on a US/UK/Commonwealth basis, towns on the visiting tour circuit such as Bath, Chester and York have historically tended to boast well-established branches. At one time the president of the Bath branch was the rather dashingly named Lt. Col. Monty Flash. Doubtless visitors were suitably impressed. For many years the Bristol branch had, as its chairman, a notable schoolteacher and television presenter named Eric Dehn, who unstintingly gave decades of service to the ESU. When interviewed for our *Journey*, Lady Dodds-Parker, a former ESU Governor and long-standing ESU supporter, fondly reminisced, 'I always sat next to Eric at meetings. He was such fun.'

Lady Heald, chairman of the Guildford branch from 1959 to 2002, used her home, Chilworth Manor, and its lovely gardens as a valuable source of fundraising and as a venue for ESU events. There were countless lunches, Christmas teas, suppers, dinners, garden parties, committee meetings and AGMs. Many musical events were held there, with such luminaries as the Yehudi Menuhin School and the Whiffenpoofs Male Choir of Yale University. Overseas visitors were warmly welcomed. With immense generosity, Lady Heald served the aims of the Guildford branch in particular and the ESU in general for forty-five years.

The Hon. Charlotte Stourton showed similar dedication. It is thought that she became a member of the ESU before the Second World War and remained one until her death, aged ninety-nine, in 2003. She was a member of firstly the Harrogate branch and subsequently the York one. She remained an active, interested and supportive member until well into her nineties. (Is there something about the ESU which encourages longevity? If so, perhaps we need to find it and bottle it.) On one occasion, she arranged for the York branch to visit her family home, Allerton Park. At the end, after a very hospitable evening, the hapless visitors – courtesy of Charlotte's navigation – became completely lost in the grounds on a moonless night. Often it is these comic episodes which last longest in memory.

Sadly Denis Rattle, Monty Flash, Eric Dehn, Lady Heald and the Hon. Charlottle Stourton are no longer with us, but their character, generosity, loyalty and dedication to the ESU are an inspiration to present and future generations.

The first ESU Branches Conference was held as far back as 1935. It was viewed as essential that branches have their own forum for generating ideas, for frank discussion and for determining their roles. The conferences provide an opportunity for members to network with their opposite numbers from fellow branches and to compare notes on common issues such as membership, event planning, obtaining speakers and other committee work.

What are the factors which go into a successful Branches Conference? ESU members comments include the following:

Actual conference events should be inside the hotel building.

Parking should be on the premises, secure and covered.

Locations should be in town centres and as close as possible to any outside arranged visits.

Other local attractions and places of interest should be in close vicinity.

Proximity to a main line railway station.

Costs kept as low as possible.

Intriguing local architecture, an excellent dinner, a lively after-dinner speech and fascinating local outings are also relevant. An enjoyable social occasion lays the groundwork for serious business to be discussed. A contemporary business slogan encourages us to 'Act local, think global' and this certainly applies to ESU branches.

For instance, shortly after the millennium, at the 2002 Branches Conference in Droitwich Spa, Worcestershire, the theme could have not have been more timely. It was 'The Resurgence and Relevance of the English-Speaking Union in the 21st Century'. Peter Sparling, outgoing chairman of the National Council for England and Wales, spoke about developments in the UK, particularly the successful establishment of the London branch and the introduction of simplified subscriptions. 'Now every member everywhere is the same, with no more distinctions between Country and Club members.' He noted that membership was rising in the UK and has been 'more than resurgent in the international sphere'. Peter then introduced the ESU chairman, Lord Watson, who spoke of the vitality of the new overseas openings and the opportunity for the ESU to bring the world closer together through new technologies and initiatives such as internet debates.

Delegates were encouraged to become more involved in raising the profile of the ESU locally. 'Move from press releases sent to neutral or hostile media to sharing with them, perhaps creating exclusives,' Lord Watson urged. Wise words indeed ... To many grassroots organisations, using the media to get their message across can seem daunting and frustrating. The reality is that local radio stations, in particular, are almost always on the lookout for interesting speakers to come in, be interviewed and contribute to lively discussions. Guests are, after all, free performers. The *quid pro quo* is that the guests get a chance to discreetly 'plug' the benefits of their organisation. Yes, you too can be a media star – well, a local one anyway.

With press releases, it is even more important to produce brief, lively stories which hard-pressed local journalists can quickly 'cut and paste' into their publications. Often local newspapers and magazines will be cash-strapped, with journalists frantically juggling a variety of roles. Press releases which 'do all the work for them' quickly rise to the top of the pile. If you understand how these media operate – and, even better, as Lord Watson suggested, you actively partner with them – your chances of getting your message across to your audience are markedly increased.

The next speaker, the then Director-General Valerie Mitchell, emphasised the value of branch support for all ESU programmes. Her praise for the following branch initiatives is as relevant today:

Providing grants and scholarships.

Raising money for overseas English teachers.

Raising money for airfares for international public speaking competitors and other international visitors.

Helping professional people, such as sponsoring nurses from overseas ESUs into UK hospitals.

Providing sponsorship for a variety of art and music scholarship programmes.

'We need the branches beyond all measure,' she affirmed. 'Probably the most important thing is the friendship and home hospitality extended by branches, which puts an extra dimension to visitors' experiences in the UK.' (It will be remembered that it was exactly this spirit of hospitality which so entranced Evelyn Wrench on his first visit to America and laid the inspiration for his founding of both the Royal Over-Seas League and the ESU.) Valerie Mitchell reminded the audience that, more than ever in the post 9/11 world, 'the ordinary things we do combat powerful fear and prejudice. We must recognise the great contribution we can make on the world stage.'

Other speakers on that day made observations and suggestions, well received and well acted upon, which remain relevant. The then Director of Education, Dr Neil Gilroy-Scott, noted that the branches have an important role to play in educational programmes such as the Schools Public Speaking Competition. With the Secondary Schools Exchange programme, he observed that 'UK students come from all classes and parents now and are more likely to be older, perhaps single parents or retired. Branches can make small grants to the students, which are enormously appreciated. They are delighted to come to branch meetings to speak about their experiences.'

And, of course, such ESU alumni provide not only intriguing tales of their time abroad, as we have seen in 'The Alumnus Experience'. Their feedback is of inestimable importance in assuring ESU members that their efforts are worthwhile.

Holly Shakespeare, then chairman of the Exeter and District branch, spoke about the approach, ethos and lessons learned in her branch's experiences of membership recruitment. It is often claimed that one of the best ways in which to be successful is to model your efforts on existing success. In the previous eight years, the Exeter branch had gone from meetings held in members' sitting rooms to a roll of more than 300. While not all of the Exeter lessons will apply everywhere, they certainly provide a useful checklist for other branches to consider. Holly's conclusions were as follows:

> All meetings were held in the same good quality venue, with alternating lunch and supper meetings, from month to month. Good food was deemed essential. Menus were chosen up to a year in advance, so members could make well-informed decisions.
>
> Ample parking was deemed essential.
>
> Much effort went into selecting attractive speakers and providing them with memorable hospitality.
>
> Invitations were sent to gap-year scholars, their parents, heads of schools with exchange students, and other people in the area who had been involved in ESU programmes.
>
> Publicity was important. For instance, the branch website had resulted in valuable membership enquiries.
>
> There was a comprehensive membership system and a dedicated committee.
>
> Members received information about the ESU. They were encouraged to go on international trips. They were shown how the branch fitted in with the national programme of scholarships and they were able to meet individual scholarship recipients.

At the heart of these guidelines lay professional organisation and good communication. The point about publicity echoed Lord Watson's thoughts. Make the media your friend, by giving it interesting, marketable stories, and you will get your message across to far more people.

Interestingly enough, an article which appeared in *ESU Branches News* shortly afterwards, noted that, 'It's hard to say what makes a typical ESU branch. One of the organisation's strengths is the diversity and character of each branch.' Undoubtedly this is the case. In an age of, at times, quite stultifying homogeneity, there is nothing homogeneous about ESU branches. They reflect the history and character of individual branch members and there is a wealth of difference between branches, albeit difference aligned to common aims.

The article went on to take the Bath and District branch as an example. It was formed in 1949, thus making it over fifty years old at the millennium. The membership was 120 and rising steadily. The branch had a distinctly international flavour, with half a dozen or so members usually taking part in ESU international events such as the official ESU openings in Romania, Georgia, Latvia and St Petersburg. At the millennium, the branch sponsored Armenian and Bulgarian art students, Czech and Russian doctors, a St Petersburg nurse and a South African social worker, as well as helping several local students to study and teach abroad. In addition, the branch had been able to provide a link between three academics from St Petersburg universities and their opposite numbers from the University of Bath.

The impetus for much of this international activity had come from close to home, with active links between the Bath branch and local educational institutions, ranging from a local primary school to the University of Bath. The chairman of the branch was also on the committee of the local Royal Commonwealth Society, whose members were invited to ESU events. Also invited to events were members of the Royal Over-Seas League. Relationships such as these mean that there is a vigorous cross-fertilisation of interests, to the benefit of all concerned.

International relationships mattered greatly. For instance, following attendance by Bath members at a new ESU branch in Romania, an impromptu visit was made to Bath by a full Romanian choir who stayed with members and gave them a delightful concert.

Holly Shakespeare's comments about the organisation of the Exeter branch were echoed in the Bath branch's policy of organising events a year in advance and spacing them judiciously, usually about a month apart. The following gives a flavour of what is on offer, courtesy of the Bath branch.

> Recently members have listened to the writer and broadcaster Bel Mooney, celebrated the accession of the Queen with royal biographer Theo Aronson, breakfasted with the mayor of Bath, heard about British convicts in Australia, entertained the First Secretary from the South African High Commission and had a hilarious canal trip on the 'Jubilee' barge, which had to be repeated after the first attempt ended in mechanical breakdown. A good time was had by all on both occasions! Our Christmas dinner was a sell-out, as was our February luncheon, with more

than seventy in attendance to hear the new Bishop of Bath and Wells. Highlights of upcoming events include the High Commissioner for Pakistan, who will address the AGM and – we hope – a garden party in the Loire Valley will take place in September. Something for everyone!

Something for everyone, indeed – this certainly seems to be a formula for success. Another oft-cited factor for success in branch events is having interesting speakers. (It should be noted that interesting writers do not necessarily make interesting readers of their work – or interesting speakers, *per se*. But, increasingly, writers know that public events are an excellent opportunity not only to market their books but to get away from the computer screen long enough to actually meet people.) And writers can have fascinating stories to tell. For instance, some years ago, Lady Teresa Waugh spoke at the Taunton branch. She candidly admitted that she was a thwarted writer at school and her parents were sent a bill for £1 for her 'wasting school paper during lessons'. Marrying into the Waugh literary 'dynasty' (husband Auberon, father-in-law Evelyn) was daunting. Nevertheless her late husband had encouraged her and been extremely supportive. As the experience of ESU programmes testifies, support at a formative stage of development can make a lifetime's difference.

By contrast, at about the same time, Lord Gawain Douglas gave a fascinating talk to the Canterbury and East Kent Branch. Lord Gawain traced his family line back to the thirteenth century, with the rather ominously named 'Black Douglas', and merrily rattled family skeletons. He is the great-nephew of the poet Lord Alfred Douglas (the infamous 'Bosie'), who so scandalised Victorian Society in 1891 by his dalliance with Oscar Wilde. The affair, which would scarcely raise an eyebrow today, caused the celebrated trial of Wilde and his subsequent incarceration in Reading Gaol.

In today's highly mobile society, it probably only takes a few key people changing location for the fortunes of branches to decline or revive. Certainly there are heartening stories of branches' fortunes which have been revived. How do you start to do this? The answer seems to be: begin from wherever you are. Some time ago, John Baxter, of the Cornwall branch, told a modest but inspiring tale of how it started to turn itself around. 'The branch was nearly dead,' he confided. 'In the first year, we had a 50% increase – from six to nine!'

In a situation such as this, every new member will be special. John cited a number of specific tactics which proved useful; these included urging members to make best use of links with their other organisations, from the RSA to the golf club, to meet a target of doubling the membership annually. (It will be remembered that Evelyn Wrench was keenly aware of the 'recruitment and retention' battle and had similar targets for improving membership levels.) The Cornwall branch rediscovered the power of a varied and interesting programme of events. A Children's Laureate attracted an audience of 300 and doubtless valuable publicity. An important by-product of using Truro School for many of their events was that notices of the events were included in mailings to parents. It is back to the point of tactical alliances with other – sympathetically minded – organisations, where each others' publicity can be used for maximum mutual benefit.

At around the same time, a similar success story was told at the Canterbury and East Kent branch. The chairman, Ann Peerless, recounted how the branch had been brought 'out of dinosaur country' when 'they only had one event – the AGM'. Change and growth had followed an energetic and varied programme, featuring a picnic in a baroness's garden, literary lunches and an appearance by local resident Michael Barry. The branch had supported a local harp player and offered a scholarship to a soprano who later became main understudy for the well-known musical, *Phantom of the Opera*.

The branch had outdone itself with support for schools, helping Shakespeare's Globe Director Patrick Spottiswoode to become involved with 180 sixth formers in Kent. It had run a public speaking study day, to help students learn how to present themselves, for example at job interviews, and 'how to speak English properly'.

'We have been accused of having too many events,' Ann admitted, 'but our members are members of everything and only go to three things a year. You have to balance the lunch brigade versus the evening brigade and so on. The way ahead is to cash in on other peoples' publicity, such as the Canterbury Festival and the Deal Festival – they publish 8,000 pamphlets that mention the ESU.'

Again it's back to the same tack of 'hitch-hiking' on other organisation's publicity, for mutual benefit.

Roger Cornwell, from the Ouse Valley branch, told the story of the *Ouse Valley Letter*. During its first nine years of existence, branch membership had hovered at around the 65-70 mark. Then, in Roger's words:

> We decided last year to do something to try to get new members. We decided in advance on our full-year programme, right though from August to May, with something each month and made a nicely printed programme – it has to look good. Then we wrote a letter to all current members saying we would very much like you to send the accompanying letter to any friends who might like to join.
>
> We had a remarkable response. From July to the following March, we went from 69 members to 105 members – a 52% increase. Since then, another 15 have joined and we expect to have 30 to 40 new members by next summer. Probably a third to a half of members got a response and 15–20 people really took it seriously. Attendance at events has risen from 25–30 to 60–90.

Once again, copying information to friends was an Evelyn Wrench tactic which worked well, back in the 1920s. Some techniques are timeless, while others are mere restatements. Yesterday's 'word of mouth' is today's 'viral marketing'. *Plus ça change …*

Back in the Ouse Valley, Roger noted that it was crucial to include details of cost when appealing for new members and to be careful about controlling these costs. 'We aim to keep maximum costs to £16,' he said. The branch had more success with Saturday lunch meetings, 'more attractive to commuters than a 7.30 weeknight meeting that starts half an hour after they get home from work'.

Strategy devolves to what works best in a particular locality. Speaking about the situation of the London branch, with almost 1,200 members, Colin McCorquodale told how the committee had concluded that social programmes that work well for others will not necessarily be successful in the capital. 'What our members really want is visits in London to sites they could not easily visit individually. We now encourage people to attend Dartmouth House social events.' Overseas links were also popular; for instance, the London branch had formed a close relationship with ESU France, exchanging visits with Paris and Anjou.

Local success stories, however modest they may be deemed by the participants, do not go unnoticed. For instance, a very important part of the highly successful 2005 Branches Conference, held in Liverpool, was the public presentation of Branch Awards. The Hardacre Trophy for the most imaginative and successful project went to the Canterbury and East Kent branch. The David Griffiths Punchbowl for best media coverage went to the Exeter and District branch. The Mrs Edward Norman-Butler Gavel was presented to the Cornwall branch for the highest percentage increase in membership. London received the membership prize for the highest recruitment total. The National Council for England and Wales (NCEW) Prize for highest net increase in members went to the Ouse Valley branch. Let's face it: we all value sympathetic feedback and we all like to receive a little recognition. Knowing that Dartmouth House cares deeply about the branches makes a huge difference.

The ESU Annual Report of 2006/7 gave the following summary of the 'state of play' with the branches.

> Membership of ESU branches in England and Wales has continued to rise every month. Branches are playing an ever-larger part in the ESU's international activities as well as running their own scholarships, supporting programmes run by Dartmouth House and offering sponsorship and hospitality. Many attract high-profile speakers and are always extremely generous with their hospitality and homestays. The branches also run the early stages of the ESU Schools Public Speaking, with approximately 500 schools talking part.

Regarding the latter activity, that year the 500 or so schools took part in nine regions. The winners of each region competed in the final, which was held at Westminster. ESU Chairman, Lord Hunt of Wirral, made a closing speech, praising the standard and encouraging the competitors to continue public speaking and debating.

The Schools Public Speaking competition is an excellent example of an ESU-sponsored activity that begins at branch level and receives national exposure. Everybody has the same chance to win; and, win or lose, everybody has the same chance to become enthralled by the power of public speaking.

It is interesting how young people become drawn into branch-sponsored ESU activity, find their lives transformed by the experience, go on to considerable professional success and repay the English-Speaking Union. For instance, with the present ESU Chairman, Lord Hunt: 'I received great support from the ESU as a young man in my twenties, which helped provide me with a wonderful foundation for the thirty years I have now spent in parliamentary and public service. I am so pleased that I now have this opportunity for continuing our long association and giving something back.'

Sponsorship of ESU programmes is wide and varied. For instance, in 2006/7 the London branch made donations to English in Action, a gap year student, two Capitol Hill students, a reception for students from America and France working in the House of Commons, overseas teachers attending the Cultural seminar, international debates and the London heats of the Schools Public Speaking competition. The Guildford branch gave a bursary to a student from Bulgaria at the Yehudi Menuhin School, financial help for a student from the then newly established ESU in Chile to study in England and a contribution towards the costs of two contestants in the International Public Speaking Competition. Obviously different branches have very different sizes and situations; in their differing ways, they all do what they can.

The ESU 1999 Annual Report had noted that 'More and more branches now get involved internationally, from initiating scholarships to giving homestays.' This trend has continued in the first decade of the twenty-first century, with ever-greater branch involvement in ESU launches abroad and ever more varied support for initiatives from all over the world. For instance, ten years later, the South Wales branch was sponsoring young people in the UK and Africa. The Colchester and North-East Essex branch was supporting the International Public Speaking Competition and an Anglo-Japanese science exchange. The Hertfordshire branch was sponsoring a Russian pianist and the Southend-on-Sea branch was entertaining students from Brazil and Mauritius. Other branches were reporting similar stories.

It is clear that ever-stronger links are being formed between UK branches and ESUs in other countries, leading to the establishment of regular exchange visits and offers of home hospitality to overseas scholars, interns and conference delegates. The involvement of individual members and their branches allows friendships to form and grow between members from different parts of the world. This is entirely as it should be.

As a charitable organisation with a much-valued membership component, the English-Speaking Union is heavily dependent upon individual and collective efforts at branch level. The development of the ESU branches – both in the UK and overseas – is fully deserving of its own history. So many people have given their time, money and, perhaps most importantly, their commitment to the ESU. While some have received official recognition, many others remain unknown. As the experiences of ESU alumni readily testify, their efforts have resulted in many thousands of lives being transformed. ESU branch members may deservedly feel proud.

9
The ESU and Globalisation

'… priceless inheritance … the foundation of a common citizenship … about the world.' (Winston Churchill)

'Whoever occupies a territory also imposes on it his own social system.' Thus spoke Joseph Stalin, who practised what he preached. In 1946 Winston Churchill, a former chairman of the ESU, coined the chilling term, 'iron curtain': 'From Stettin in the Baltic to Trieste in the Adriatic, an iron curtain has descended across the Continent. Beyond that line … all are subject in one form or another, not only to Soviet influence but to a very high and, in many cases, increasing measure of control from Moscow.'

Nowhere was that iron curtain more visible than the infamous Berlin Wall which symbolised the stark division between communism and democracy. In 1963, shortly before his untimely death, President Kennedy visited Berlin. With searching honesty, he spoke thus: 'Freedom has many difficulties and democracy is not perfect, but we have never had to put a wall up to keep our people in, to prevent them from leaving us.'

To many, it must have seemed impossible that the iron curtain would ever be breached. Yet in 1989 the Berlin Wall was torn down. With the collapse of the Soviet Union, many countries found themselves seeking freedom from the rigid control of which Churchill had spoken more than forty years previously. The entire world was swept by a hitherto unprecedented wave of globalisation. In the early 1960s Marshall McLuhan had anticipated a 'global village' where improved communication – particularly electronic communication – would render physical distance between countries far less important. In the 1970s an obscure technology was developed – a network of computers with an odd name, the internet. In the 1990s and beyond, the huge growth of the internet provided a key technology of globalisation. Many years before, Stalin had caustically noted, 'Ideas are more powerful than guns. We would not let our enemies have guns; why should we let them have ideas?' It seems a safe bet that Stalin would not have approved of the freedom of the internet.

In 1989 the English-Speaking Union was seventy-one years old with ESUs in fourteen countries; in the following twenty years ESUs were opened in forty more countries. These figures speak for themselves. The challenge of that hitherto unprecedented wave of globalisation was fully taken up. Country after country realised that English was their 'cultural passport' to the world stage. The English-Speaking Union helped dozens of such counties enhance their cultural passports.

Certainly 1989 was a break-point. But to fully understand globalisation – and the key roles of the English language and of democracy – we must go back nearly 400 years to 1606. In his illuminating book *Jamestown*, subtitled *The Voyage of English*, Lord Watson, Chairman Emeritus of the International Council of the English-Speaking Union, takes us through the events of the early 1600s. In December 1606 three small ships set sail from Blackwell, near London. After a fearful voyage, in April 1607 they landed in Chesapeake Bay, at a site they named Jamestown, in 'Virginia, earth's only paradise ...' Over the next fifteen years, courtesy of the Virginia Company, 10,000 settlers arrived in Jamestown. Only 2,000 survived. From these most inauspicious of beginnings, the English language had arrived in America.

In the early 1600s there were some four million people living in England. This population comprised the greater part of the English-speaking world. Compare the situation today, with some 400 million native English speakers and around two billion of a world population of nearly eight billion able to speak English. How did English achieve such an astonishing ascendancy?

In his *History of the English-Speaking Peoples*, Churchill gave figures for the British Diaspora of the nineteenth century: 'In the 1820s [there were] a quarter of a million emigrants, in the 1830s half a million, by the middle of the century a million and a half, until, sixty-five years after Waterloo, no fewer than eight million had left the British Isles.'

It is estimated that between 1830 and 1930 over seven million people emigrated from Britain to the US. In the same timeframe, perhaps four times as many came from the rest of Europe. In the 1580s, when Queen Elizabeth I first granted Sir Walter Raleigh a warrant to plant colonies in the New World, it was realised that no such colony could long survive unless 'it could communicate with an indigenous friendly population'. Wave upon wave of emigrants, with an ever-increasing Babel of languages and dialects, served to emphasise the crucial need for a common voice. Although both Greek and German were proposed, English was finally adopted. With its adoption as the official language of the USA, the number of English speakers multiplied. John Quincy Adams saw English as a key facilitator of the rise of the USA as a great power. English would become 'the most universally read and spoken language in the world' and 'more generally the language of the world than Latin was or French is in the present age'.

In his *Dissertations on the English Language*, Adams's contemporary Noah Webster confidently predicted; 'Within a century and a half, North America will be peopled with 100 million men all speaking the same language. Compare this prospect with the state of the English language in Europe, almost confined to an island and to a few million people.'

As the British Diaspora gained pace, English became widely spoken not only in America but also in Canada, Australia, New Zealand, South Africa and the West Indies. It was also used significantly throughout North Africa and Asia, particularly India. By 1930 there were more people in the US of British origin – some 75 million – than there were in Britain.

English, as an intellectual property, had been exported first to America and then to much of the remainder of the world. Hand-in-hand with English went the concepts of law, individual freedom and free enterprise. The German statesman Bismarck rightly predicted that the most profound influence in history would be 'the fact that the North Americans speak English'. But of course it was not the mere fact of dozens of millions of people speaking a common tongue; it was also the fact that these same dozens of millions of people had also embraced the concepts of law, individual freedom and free enterprise. As Patrick Wormald, author of *The Making of English Law,* sagely noted, 'English language and law are the most enduring marks of Englishness, its main claims to anyone else's attention.' Magna Carta gave a legal code, however partial. Magna Carta's intellectual descendent, the Declaration of Independence has, as Lord Watson points out, 'never been bettered as the justification of the state and the object of politics'. The simple fact is that, irrespective of culture or political outlook, 'life, liberty and the pursuit of happiness' have immense resonance with the human spirit.

The second decade of the twentieth century saw a huge challenge to the English-Speaking peoples – the First World War. Evelyn Wrench witnessed the consequent joining together of America, Britain and the Dominions in armed conflict. In 1918 Churchill declared 'a great harmony' between the 'spirit and language of the Declaration of Independence and all that we are fighting for now'. For him the Declaration of Independence had crucial importance: 'It followed on Magna Carta and the Bill of Rights as the third great title deed on which the liberties of the English speaking people are founded.' The First World War was between 'nations where peoples own governments and nations where the governments own peoples'.

We have seen how, in 1918, Evelyn Wrench realised that this new-found alignment of America, Britain and the Dominions provided the best hope for world peace. Seizing the day, founding the English-Speaking Union, was his masterstroke, an act of genius. The 'spirit and language' of democracy and of human freedom would be preserved through international friendship.

Undoubtedly the Second World War proved the greatest challenge of the twentieth century to democracy and human freedom. For historian Stephen Bungay, 'If Britain had given up in 1940, the war could have had only one of two possible outcomes: Nazi or Soviet domination of Europe.' Churchill proved the truth of Stalin's stark axiom, 'Ideas are more powerful than guns.' With a use of the English language which will probably never be bettered, he affirmed the crucial, undying importance of liberty. In his 1961 inaugural address, President Kennedy echoed Churchill's wartime sentiment: 'Let every nation know, whether it wishes us well or ill, that we shall pay any price, bear any burden, meet any hardship, support any friend, oppose any foe, in order to assure the survival and the success of liberty.'

For Stalin, 'A single death is a tragedy; a million deaths is a statistic.' In the Second World War when, terribly, it was necessary to 'pay any price', over 60 million people died. Stalin was utterly wrong. These deaths are no cold statistic; they are 60 million tragedies. At stake was 'the right of all peoples to choose the form of government under which they will live'. No more fundamental right may be envisaged.

For Churchill, during the Second World War, English was not only a means of conveying 'ideas ... more powerful than guns'. It was also a 'priceless inheritance' which might, in a future peacetime, 'become the foundation of a common citizenship'. It would be such 'a grand convenience for us all to be able to move freely about the world and be able to find everywhere a medium ... of intercourse and understanding'. Might this medium – English – 'not also be an advantage to many races and an aid to the building up of our new structure for preserving peace?' Churchill was re-stating Wrench's vision of 1918. As Lord Watson points out, he was also making another visionary leap in identifying English as the medium of further waves of globalisation.

The end of the Second World War signalled the beginning of the Cold War between East and West, communism and capitalism. The calamitous defeat of the French at Dien Bien Phu in 1954 spelled the beginning of the end of colonialism. The Suez crisis of 1956 reinforced that message. During the following decades, country after country gained independence. Flags of newly independent states, such as Ghana and Malaya, were proudly displayed in Dartmouth House. Meanwhile, behind the iron curtain, rigid control prevailed, courtesy of a nexus of police states. But there is only so long that the human spirit can be repressed. In 1989 the Berlin Wall finally fell. Countries such as Poland, Hungary, Bulgaria, Czechoslovakia and Romania all chose freedom. In the final decade of the twentieth century, globalisation received a huge boost.

It is currently estimated that, just over twenty years after the fall of the Berlin Wall, about 50% of the world's population is under the age of thirty. This huge tranche of people has grown up with globalisation as the dominant imperative of their lives. Some 30% of the world's population speak English. In the twentieth century, English was the dominant language of three truly global communications media: movies, rock music and the internet. Generations of young people learned English not because they were forced to, but because English was their personal 'cultural passport' to a world of increasingly interactive media. In the 1960s, listening to the radio or watching television enabled people to understand the world. In the early years of the present century, putting your home-made videos on to the internet enables people to *create* their worlds. At its most fundamental, using English means that your message will probably reach dozens, hundreds, perhaps thousands of times more people.

As our world has coalesced into the predicted 'global village', the drive for instant communication has become relentless. We may applaud a rich diversity of languages, dialects and cultures but, pragmatically, we need a common tongue. English is the preferred language of technical domains such as air traffic control. It is the principal language of many multinationals, irrespective of their origins. Over 70% of scientific and medical theses are in English. In the European Union, it is the preferred second language of 85% of all EU officials. For Queen Elizabeth II, the Patron of the English-Speaking Union, English is 'the golden thread' of the Commonwealth.

So globalisation is no mere *fin de siècle* phenomenon. Its roots go back hundreds of years to the founding of that great global melting pot that became America. English was adopted as the official language not from sentiment but from pragmatism. However English came as part of a 'cultural package' which also included personal liberty protected by legal rights. Despite the severe challenges posed by both world wars, the international appetite for English – and its concomitants, democracy, legality and freedom – has grown at a ferocious rate. The Berlin Wall was torn down in 1989 because the human spirit has always – and will always - yearn for 'life, liberty and the pursuit of happiness'.

As we have seen, back in 1919, just after the formation of the ESU, there was an internal debate about 'Definition of the term "English-Speaking" as regards eligibility for membership'. 'The Central Committee noted that: 'Dr Muirhead's suggestion that "English-Speaking" should mean British subjects whose mother-tongue was English was received, but it was decided not to draw up any definite rules, and to decide each case on its merits.'

Behind this resolution 'not to draw up any definite rules', one senses the invisible hand of Evelyn Wrench, anxious that the spirit of the ESU should not be stifled so soon after birth. The citizens of the United States of America, which joined the ESU in 1920, were hardly 'British subjects'. The whole point of the ESU was to bridge cultural chasms. Deciding each case on its merits paved the way for Bermuda, Australia, New Zealand and Canada becoming early joiners of the ESU.

'Of course Wrench was an Anglo-American fellow' is a sentiment which is often uttered. But was he *merely* an Anglo-American fellow? The evidence suggests not. As we have seen, back in the early 1920s, there is a tantalising reference to a visit by Wrench to Paris regarding the proposed opening of a French branch. A suggestion that the ESU open in Belgium received enthusiastic approval by Wrench. A lady wrote to offer her support. 'You ask me if I can help you when you establish a branch in Japan. I shall be glad to do anything I can ...'

The Second World War changed the role of the ESU first to that of an aid organisation, and then to a hospitality organisation. Had the war not intervened, would the ESU have 'gone global' in the 1940s? It is one of those tantalising 'what ifs' of history. After the war, the ESU concentrated on internal matters such as massively improving and expanding its educational programmes, courtesy of the inimitable duo of Lillian Moore and Yvonne Theobald. Sir Evelyn Wrench devoted himself to writing. Both as a man of ideas and as a man of action, he always worked for the greater good.

Scotland joined the ESU in 1952 and Pakistan joined in 1961. Both were most welcome additions. Probably the next driver for the ESU's globalisation was Britain joining the European Union in the 1970s. At that time, to certain of its governors, the ESU was a long-standing Anglo-American and Commonwealth organisation. To others, expanding into Europe was not only in alignment with the spirit of the times; it was a long-overdue move. The then Director-General, Hugh Jones, was in favour of such expansion and suggested Brussels, a multilingual city destined to become the hub of European politics. A highly capable intermediary, John Szemerey, facilitated the opening of an ESU in Brussels – the first such ESU on mainland Europe. A template for many other ESUs, both in Europe and elsewhere, was established. Rightly Jones has lauded Szemerey as 'an outstanding ESU pioneer'.

In 1980 Nigeria became the first ESU to be established in Africa. In the early 1980s Sri Lanka and India became the first ESUs to be established in Asia. The 1980s also saw ESUs established in Germany, France and Austria. The relatively early entry of France into 'the ESU family' was very much facilitated by the efforts of Madame Beatrix de Montgermont-Keil, whose efforts in Europe on behalf of the ESU show that the *entente cordiale* is alive and well. The French launch was held with a grand dinner in the Senate Presidential rooms. It was hosted by Pierre-Christian Taittinger, Vice-President of the French Senate, Honorary President of ESU France and a member of the famous champagne-producing family.

In 2007 another dinner was held at The Jockey Club in Paris to celebrate the twentieth anniversary of ESU France. Reminiscences included the following:

'When ESU France was founded twenty years ago everyone thought it remarkable, if not hazardous. Now it seems self-evident that the ESU should be here in France and doing so well in France.'

Undoubtedly France, which has brought three branches into the ESU fold, is a great success story. Representing France at the eighty-fifth anniversary of the ESU, Madame Beatrix de Montgermont-Keil was 'so proud to fly the flag of France in Westminster Abbey'.

In 1988 the ESU celebrated its seventieth birthday. Its chairman was the newly arrived Lord Pym, the former Defence Secretary, Leader of the House and Foreign Secretary. Lord Pym was certainly a good man to have in a tight spot. In 1945 he had earned a Military Cross in Italy. In 1982, as Defence Secretary during the Falklands war, he brought to the office calm, precision, shrewdness and diplomacy. In the late 1980s the ESU was struggling to overcome financial difficulties and renovate Dartmouth House. Lord Pym was ably backed by deputy chairman, Lady Luce, who also succeeded him as acting chairman pending the appointment of Baroness Brigstocke. For Lady Luce, Lord Pym gave 'superb leadership'. She was unequivocal in her support for Dartmouth House: 'A major issue was the proposed sale of Dartmouth House, in which I became deeply involved. I was strongly against the sale. In economic terms it seemed a nonsense to sell two freeholds in the centre of Mayfair.'

For Lady Luce, Dartmouth House was 'the best and cheapest club-house in Mayfair', a place where 'visitors ... will always find something they wish to become involved in – provided they are interested in working with (and for) people – that is the key.' In addition to promoting understanding and friendship, for Lady Luce the ESU also had a role to play in promoting events: 'The success of the Churchill Lecture, the Cambridge cultural seminar and the Summer Conference shows there is a demand for well organised and well presented events.'

The ESU had superb assets to deploy. In concert with Lady Luce, Lord Pym led initiatives for renovation and increased scholarship programmes. Branches and membership increased. A seventieth anniversary at Dartmouth House was attended by the ESU's President, The Duke of Edinburgh, and 300 guests. The US Ambassador, The Hon. Henry Catto, made his first official UK appearance at the Branches Conference. Writing in the ESU journal, *Concord*, David Hicks recorded: 'Not the least of our assets is a strong and wise Chairman, Francis Pym, whose influence got President Reagan to give this year's Churchill Lecture and so enhanced our standing considerably.'

At the World Conference in Ottawa, on 'English and World Communications' Lord Pym made a speech on 'Propagating the Use of English' in which he suggested that the global village needed a language and pointed out that one billion people spoke English. In 1991, as guest of honour and speaker at the Branches Conference in Liverpool, he articulated a renewed spirit of optimism for the ESU:

> We can help to unite this troubled world by the use of English, which has grown into the international language, and this underlines the significance of the ESU. At this time of resurgence and renewal, when political barriers are coming down, there is, in spite of the problems in the Middle East, a sense of optimism in the air which can be developed through a partnership of commerce, industry and individuals.

These were prescient words. The same year, 1991, marked an important watershed with the opening of the first ESU in Eastern Europe – Serbia Montenegro. Yugoslavia (the land of the South Slavs) had been created, post-First World War, by a merger of largely Catholic areas of Slovenia and Croatia with the Eastern Orthodox areas of Serbia and Montenegro. The merger also included Bosnia, with Catholic Croat, Orthodox Serb and Muslim Slav populations respectively. Despite deep ethnic, religious and cultural divisions, integration lasted until the Second World War, when a combined German/Italian invasion triggered civil war. Following the war, the communist dictator, Josip Broz Tito, reunited Yugoslavia – with an iron fist. Dissension was not tolerated and the nation returned to the appurtenance of political stability. However this enforced stability hid an 'ethnic time bomb'. With Tito's death in 1980, it was only a matter of time before the inevitable political explosions. In 1991 came the first of what would be many such explosions when the Serbian politician Slobodan Milosevic came to power. Slovenia and Croatia declared independence. Serbs living in southern and western Croatia attempted to break away, to form a new nation called Krajina. In 1992 Bosnia broke away from Yugoslavia, precipitating yet another war. In southern Yugoslavia, Macedonia also broke away, thankfully relatively peacefully.

Thus, in 1991, Serbia Montenegro, despite an illustrious history, was the newest of nation states. What do you do with a raw nation state uncomfortably close to civil war? The ESU ethos is to give what help it can, if that help is sought and if it seems that such help will be productive. Was it wanted? In the words of Branka Panic, Chairman of ESU Serbia: 'You have no idea how much this ESU means to our people in Belgrade. You are the country of democracy and peace. You are the light that gives us the confidence to go forward.'

Understandably, until the 1990s, most ESUs were established in an *ad hoc* manner, best fitting the circumstances. However in the post-1989 world it rapidly became apparent that a more systematic approach needed to be adopted. As any seasoned diplomat will assure you, it is all too easy to fall foul of a culture and history whose hidden depths you cannot possibly comprehend. In such situations, proffered solutions can quickly become enmeshed in long-standing problems.

To avoid such malaises it was necessary to adopt a strategic approach to setting up ESUs. Accordingly the then Chairman, Baroness Brigstocke, and the then Director-General, Valerie Mitchell, devised the modestly entitled *Guidelines for Setting Up an ESU*. The ESU should always act in concert with the Foreign and Commonwealth Office, with its unique appreciation of the cultural and political climate. And it should also act in concert with the British Council, which almost invariably has highly relevant expertise. With twenty years of hindsight, it is clear that this tripartite approach has avoided pitfalls and reaped rewards. Back in 1910, when Evelyn Wrench was setting up the Royal Over-Seas Club, he realised the key importance of having charismatic leadership in each country. Eighty years later, *Guidelines for Setting Up an ESU* stressed the importance both of charismatic leadership and the delicate skills of forming and running a committee. Prospective ESU leaders visit England, meet with the Director-General and receive eminently practical help and support in setting up their ESU. Thus the prospects for the new ESU are markedly improved.

Serbia had been the ESU's initial foray into Eastern Europe, followed by Bulgaria and Romania. In December 1989 Romania had overthrown the Ceausescu government. In the 1990s the country was in extremely difficult circumstances. It will be readily appreciated that, at such times, any outside organisation, no matter how well intentioned, must be doubly careful. Thus the strategic approach of Foreign and Commonwealth Office/British Council liaison; and thus the importance of following the *Guidelines for Setting Up an ESU*.

Romania was notable for another reason. It was the first ESU opening with significant membership attendance. There were over 150 members present, representing ESUs from half a dozen countries. The members were overwhelmed by the hospitality shown them. There are cherished memories of 'an amazing launch, with bouquets of flowers for everyone. We travelled around in Bucharest in VIP London taxis.' There was even 'The ESU Song' especially written for the occasion.

In the blunt words of Dr Veronica Focseneanu, Chairman of ESU Romania-Bucharest, and composer of 'The ESU Song', 'If we are going to survive, we have to learn English.' And this is undoubtedly the case. But it would be wrong to think that such ESU openings are simply about economic survival – desperately important though this is. Sadly Romania is a country where contact with much of the outside world had been prohibited for many years. In such circumstances, you want to reach out to other people, to affirm both their humanity and yours. It is, perhaps, the national equivalent of having been wrongfully imprisoned for decades and suddenly stepping into the light as a free person. Just being able to sit and drink coffee with a friend – something which all of us take for granted every day of our lives – becomes a hitherto unimaginable luxury.

Many readers of this book will have had the experience of going to out-of-the way places, well off the beaten track, where the inhabitants have little of material value. So often, the visitor is overwhelmed by the warmth of hospitality. Thus the ESU members were overwhelmed by the warmth of hospitality shown to them in Romania. We are reminded that capitalism needs to be enlightened, not soulless, that giving help to others and receiving help from others is an affirmation of our deepest humanity. Some 3,000 years ago, Phoenician sailors made long, perilous journeys, meeting many races in many countries, making friends, and trading with them for mutual benefit. It is still a wise example for today.

Interestingly a 1990s ESU Churchill Lecture given by the distinguished academic Lord Dahrendorf reached much the same conclusion. Responding to Baroness Brigstocke's invitation, Lord Dahrendorf analysed our 'modern predicament' and asked whether the three main characteristics of our way of life – freedom, civil responsibility and prosperity – can possibly be compatible. Internationalisation has become a fact of economic life; yet it is all too easy for our senses of community and responsibility towards others to be eroded. 'Can we square the circle successfully and be prosperous and civil too?' Lord

Dahrendorf asked. He concluded that, at least in Europe, the answer was yes – but only if we revitalised our society by giving more power to local initiatives and by encouraging voluntary activity and charitable action. Lord Dahrendorf concluded that we can be truly prosperous *only* if we are civil.

Branch involvement in the Romanian launch had marked a turning point in international development. Subsequent involvement gave ESU branches a renewed *raison d'être*. When you are personally involved in activities which are transforming peoples' lives, suddenly fundraising events become charged with a renewed sense of purpose. Invariably it is a two-way process. In helping others, you are helped yourself, sometimes in quite subtle ways. Ultimately all of us must review our lives. We must ask ourselves, as did Evelyn Wrench, 'What is the best use of my precious time on earth?' For many of us, a key component of our 'best destiny' will be helping others and receiving help in return.

Appropriately 1996 saw an ESU World Members' Conference entitled 'English – World Language, Global Opportunities'. It was the first such conference to have been held in England in twenty years. Over 300 delegates, representing twenty-seven countries, took part. Speakers included Lord Quirk and Professor David Crystal. The event was enlivened by talks from Eric Dehn, doyen of the Bristol branch, and Terry Waite, who had previously held book launches at Dartmouth House. There was a renewed resolution about the ESU, a sense that, towards the end of the twentieth century, its purpose had never been more compellingly relevant. Across the Atlantic, the baton of Chairman of the English-Speaking Union of the United States passed from J. Sinclair Armstrong to William R. Miller, OBE, who later also became Chairman of the International Council. Both men brought great ability to their roles; we are in their debt.

1998 saw ESUs established in Russia, in both Moscow and St Petersburg. The official ceremony was attended by over 100 people, including the British Ambassador. Following the dissolution of much of the former Soviet empire, Russia had also endured a troubled decade, with professors being forced to moonlight as taxi drivers in order to feed their families. The Russian population has endured so much pain for so long. It is estimated that in the Second World War over 20 million people died. The tragedy is that, despite huge natural resources, by far the principal resource in Russia is its people. Although much has been accomplished in Russia, equally much remains. The Russian people deserve prosperity and the ESU has a role to play in helping them attain it.

In 1999 an ESU was launched in Brazil, surely destined to become a major world player. Despite all its social problems, Brazil has the world's eighth largest economy. The turn of the century also marked the end of the charismatic Baroness Brigstocke's tenure as Chairman of the English-Speaking Union. In six years, she had left her mark on country after country. Her place was taken by Lord Watson – a power-house of enthusiasm.

Different people, different personalities, each of them working in tandem, realising the same vision ... The 2003 ESU launch in Mongolia was 'a magical and unforgettable experience'. For Valerie Mitchell, it was 'one of the greatest experiences of my life'. Travelling from Russia into Asia and onwards to Ulan Bator, it may be that, at times, the ESU delegates unwittingly followed in the footsteps of Evelyn Wrench a hundred years before. Representatives from five countries spoke at the official launch. Exquisite music was played on horse-hair fiddles. Visits were made to Buddhist monasteries and temples. Once again there was a sense of a country opening up great cultural richness to the world. And there was a sense of people from very different cultures coming together to celebrate both difference and unity.

From Mongolia to Lebanon – the first ESU opening in the Middle East. Lebanon has been part of the cradle of civilisation for thousands of years. More recently, its devastation by war has evoked mixed emotions of sympathy and respect that it endures as such a formidable banking and commercial centre. To stand in the centre of Beirut and see the former 'Paris of the Middle East' being restored to its former splendour, literally brick by brick, is a humbling sight. To reflect that this restoration is being done sometimes for the second, or the third, or even the fourth time, is to glimpse something of the immense resilience of the Lebanese people.

It was at this time that the ESU's mission statement became 'Creating global understanding through English'. Romania, Russia, Brazil, Mongolia ... and so many other countries in between. The mission had to be global. The whole world was changing and the ESU was an integral agent of this change.

On 26 June 2003 the ESU celebrated its eighty-fifth anniversary at Westminster Abbey, where in 1910, at the funeral of King Edward VII, the course of Evelyn Wrench's life had so dramatically altered. Winston

Churchill had 'armed the English language' in the defence of world liberty. Dartmouth House had contributed to the war effort. The ESU had touched the lives of tens of thousands of people. In Lord Watson's words: 'And in its turn the ESU has been enriched by all these people, gaining from their perspectives, thrilled by their enthusiasm, energised by their grasp of wider horizons for themselves and others.'

Alluding to the surge in globalisation, he said:

> Since the fall of the Berlin Wall in 1989, the ESU's expansion in East and Central Europe has responded to an imperative need to build bridges of contact, understanding and opportunity. In Asia and Latin America, the ESU's growth nurtures understanding between peoples and generations at a crucial moment in world development.

A warm welcome was given to the latest arrivals to the ESU 'family':

> Our two newest ESUs are here in the Abbey today – the Lebanon and Madagascar. Both countries know themselves to face daunting challenges but, in both, people believe the English language and the ESU can help to release human potential and provide vital links to the global community.

In the words of the then ESU Director-General, Valerie Mitchell:

> From the first glimpse of the English-Speaking Union flag flying over Westminster Abbey to the joyous sound of the bells pealing over Westminster, the Service of Thanksgiving to celebrate eighty-five years of the ESU proved to be an unforgettable experience for all who attended: the words, the music, the spectacular procession of flags representing thirty-three countries of the ESU with the extravagant and vibrant national costumes of the flag-bearers all confirming the idealism, the commitment and global appeal of the English-Speaking Union. It was a colourful and thrilling sight.

During the following years, the first decade of the new century, the globalisation of the ESU continued apace. Finland and Russia were joined by Georgia. Latvia was joined by Estonia. Malaysia, Thailand and Vanuatu were joined by the Philippines. Argentina and Brazil were joined by Chile and Mexico. Japan was joined by Korea. Poland was joined by the Czech Republic. Morocco was joined by Lebanon and

Cyprus. Armenia was joined by Moldova and Albania. Mauritius was joined by Madagascar. Sri Lanka was joined by Hong Kong.

Few would argue with the assertion that China is set to become a world superpower in the twenty-first century. In the first decade the continuing rise of China has been the top media story in the world. During his November 2009 visit, President Obama referred to China's playing a larger role in global events as one of the most important trends of the last two decades. President Obama welcomed this trend and affirmed the US desire to become an effective partner.

In 1939 Winston Churchill had memorably described Russia as '... a riddle, wrapped in a mystery, inside an enigma'. For most people, then and since, China has seemed even more enigmatic. In December 2009, just a month after President Obama's visit, ESU alumnus Madame Fu Ying, the Chinese ambassador to Britain, was the guest speaker at the ESU's annual Churchill Lecture. It was attended by Mary, Baroness Soames, the daughter of Sir Winston. Madame Fu Ying began by thanking the ESU 'for giving me a unique training course in Oxford for speaking and debating skill during my study in UK'. Twenty-four years previously, as an unknown student, the ESU had supported her. In 2009, as Chinese ambassador, she was gracefully giving back, not only to the ESU but to everyone in the assembled audience.

The theme of Madame Fu Ying's Churchill Lecture, 'Understanding China', could not have been more relevant. She pointed out that, in the thirteen years since 1996, the Chinese economy had grown twenty times. It is now the third largest economy in the world. The national wealth created in one day in 2008 was larger than the entire annual output for 1952. With only 7% of the world's arable land to feed 20% of the world's population, China had used its new-found wealth to lift 250 million people out of poverty.

Madame Fu Ying unashamedly told us that, throughout China's long and illustrious history, food had always been of great concern. She recalled that, until the 1980s, Chinese people would greet each other by asking 'Have you had your meal?' Wryly she divulged that 'for my daughter's generation, if you greet them in this way, they might think you have a problem ...'

With commendable honesty, Madame Fu Ying noted that, despite enormous economic triumph, there were no grounds for complacency. Instead, there were 'domestic concerns and challenges' for this fast-developing nation. 'We in China are more conscious of our weaknesses and the challenges facing our country.' The economic vibrancy of the big cities had to be extended to the regions. The living standards of so many had to rise. 'China's difficult mission is to enable all of our 1.3 billion people to have the opportunity to realise their dreams.' China has almost 18% of the world's population. One person in six is Chinese. The future of China is integral to the future of the world.

Madame Fu Ying spoke of English as a key component of China's desire to embrace the world. She told us that, each year, 20 million more Chinese people begin learning English. In China, there are 2,000 newspapers and 9,000 magazines. Nearly a quarter of a million books are published annually. There are 360 million internet users. As Madame Fu Ying put it, 'So there is a very lively public expressing their views – sometimes positive and sometimes critical – on almost everything.' Increasingly these views are being expressed in English ... Is there useful work for the ESU to do in China? Almost certainly.

2010 began with the opening of ESU Bangladesh. Interestingly this came about partly through the efforts of Professor Alan Lee Williams, a former Director-General of the ESU. Currently Professor Williams is chairman of the Sir William Beveridge Foundation, a UK-based international charity which exists to alleviate practical and social problems arising from poverty.

> At the core is its desire to show how, in providing people with the right tools and the right support where and when they need it, they can be encouraged to live a life that includes hope, dignity, confidence and self-esteem coupled with an ability to care about and help others.

The Beveridge Foundation is active in Bangladesh, a heavily populated country which has been severely afflicted by natural disasters. As with China, Bangladesh has a rich history; in both countries, civilisations flourished thousands of years before remotely comparable developments in Europe. It is highly likely that, as with China, Bangladesh will become a key player in the world economy; right now, however, help is needed. Bengali people are fiercely patriotic; Bangla, their first language, is a prized emblem of national identity and National Language Month is universally celebrated.

It is much to the credit of Professor Williams, Mr Asif A. Chowdhury and Major General Jiban Kanai Das that, in Bangladesh, the ethos of the ESU coincides so amicably with that of the Beveridge Foundation.

Few would argue with the proposition that English is one of 'the right tools' for international trade and international friendship. As ever, the ESU is mindful that English should delicately complement indigenous language. With an established platform of public speaking in schools and with the support of the business community in Dhaka, it seems likely that the opening of the ESU in Bangladesh will result in considerable educational and practical benefit.

Following on from the opening of the Bangladesh ESU came openings in Malta and Turkey respectively. In the words of Martin Scicluna, chairman of ESU Malta: 'Given the importance of English to Malta's development in business, commerce, financial services and tourism, the establishment of the English-Speaking Union of Malta is seen as a crucial step forward.'

A similar rationale applies in Turkey where Chairman Riza Kadilar brought sound business expertise, prior experience of setting up non-governmental organisations and, not least, charismatic flair to the ESU launch. In both countries, debating and public speaking programmes have enjoyed considerable success. The respective business communities realise the professional importance of English.

Although age should never be a barrier to learning a new language, probably the easiest time to learn is when you are young.

> In addition [Martin Scicluna said], we started an initiative in October 2009 to introduce a practical, hands-on English-speaking support programme, 'Arm of Support', starting with the Zabbar Primary School, a state school in a relatively disadvantaged part of Malta. Here, over the last twelve months, just under 180 children, aged three and four years, have been very successfully and enthusiastically exposed to English conversation through play activities under the guidance of our volunteer teachers and in close collaboration with English teachers at Zabbar School. The project received glowing reports from the University Faculty of Literacy, which carried out an assessment of the effects of our work in the first year. We plan to extend the 'Arm of Support' programme to another school starting next month.

Successful openings of ESUs in Bangladesh, in Malta and in Turkey require not only appropriate processes of due diligence but also ones of meeting mutual expectations. Successful launch ceremonies depend upon a great deal of hard work, behind the scenes. The hard – but highly rewarding – work continues afterwards. As Martin Scicluna succinctly puts it: 'Underpinning all of these efforts is our awareness that they must be based on solid administrative and financial foundations.' As ever, the assistance of the Foreign and Commonwealth Office (FCO) and the British Council is gratefully acknowledged.

In 1989 the English-Speaking Union was seventy-one years old, with ESUs in fourteen countries. In the following twenty years, ESUs were opened in forty more countries. With some 192 countries in the world, to go from 7% representation to 28% representation is remarkable. Such 'market penetration' would make any business guru green with envy. The credit for such success must be shared among many people – not least the respective chairmen, Lord Pym, Lady Luce, Baroness Brigstocke, Lord Watson and Lord Hunt. From 1990 to 1994 as Deputy Director-General and from 1994 to 2009 as Director-General, Valerie Mitchell lent an enviable continuity to this globalisation 'explosion'. In her words: 'We never forced ourselves on countries – but, if they needed help, we were there for them. And we never launched an ESU in a country without the blessing of the Foreign and Commonwealth Office and the British Council.'

With the establishment of ESUs in 28% of the world's countries, an amazing infrastructure has been put in place. Many more countries are tentatively emerging onto the world stage. They too require 'cultural passports'. Each nation needs recognition from fellow nations. Each nation needs investment. And, at times, each nation, whether tiny or huge, needs sympathy, help and support. English has been freely chosen by the world as the medium of global understanding. The lesson is clear: if you want recognition, investment, sympathy, support or help, then it's probably a good idea to ask in English.

A complementary challenge is to build upon the established infrastructure. To encourage interaction between ESUs in different countries is to invest the globalisation of the English-Speaking Union with a richness, both economic and cultural, in which all will benefit.

10
The Future of The English-Speaking Union

'The world ... is in the midst of troubled times and difficulties, however dire, have a silver lining. The English-Speaking Union is that silver lining.'
(Valerie Mitchell)

The English-Speaking Union was founded in 1918. Thus its 100th anniversary falls due in 2018. Accordingly some may find our '*Journey*' slightly premature. But there are reasons – sound reasons – for writing this '*Journey*' in 2010 (and it will be extremely interesting to update it in eight years' time.)

The first reason is that, as previously noted, the last twenty years, following the collapse of the Berlin Wall, have seen a tremendous wave of globalisation – and an equally tremendous response by the ESU. Undoubtedly this wave of globalisation will continue. Nevertheless this is a good time to stand back and take stock.

Another reason is that we have reached the end of the first decade of the twenty-first century. World problems – and possibilities – may be very different indeed in this new century. It is possible that, by the end of it, the human race will have travelled as far as it did in the previous millennium. The searing rate of change is here to stay. Our problem – both as individuals and organisations – is how to keep up with it. So, if the ESU is to springboard from twentieth to twenty-first century success, we need to consider key elements of world change.

A third reason is that there are changes of leadership in the ESU. For twenty years, firstly as Deputy Director-General and latterly as Director-General, Valerie Mitchell has spearheaded international development. Now, with Mike Lake as Director-General, it is an opportune time to review. We need to ask the most fundamental of questions. Where have we been? Where are we now? What is our future?

The previous chapters of our '*Journey*' have answered the first question. The heady days of 1918 saw the realisation of the shared vision of Evelyn Wrench and Walter Hines Page. It is important to remember once again that, then as now, the US/UK relationship had its detractors on both sides of the Atlantic. Again, in the build-up to the Second World War, there was the same species of detractors. As we have seen, in an early issue of *The Landmark* back in the 1920s, Evelyn Wrench comprehensively answered the detractors of that era. Wrench's rich and varied mailbox testified to a widespread 'friendship across the ocean'. That friendship had already been tested in the First World War and would later be tested in the Second. On both occasions, British, American and Commonwealth service-people and civilians made major sacrifices for a peace which is all too often taken for granted today. In 1918 Wrench instinctively felt that the best chance of world peace lay in a deepening relationship between the US and the UK. Governments rise and fall, politicians come and go but, looking back over the last ninety years of world history, it is clear that Wrench was utterly correct in his political vision.

As Wrench and Lord Northcliffe discussed the formation of the English-Speaking Union on the last day of June 1918, they could hear the guns across the Channel. No more poignant reminder of the need for world peace could be envisaged.

Almost from Wrench's earliest days, he seems to have had a remarkable degree of what we might now term 'tolerance of ambiguity'. In a bitterly divisive Ireland, Wrench found no difficulty whatsoever in seeing the other person's point of view. And, even when he disagreed, there is no sense of rancour on either side. He appears to have remained on excellent terms with everyone. Firstly in Ireland, and then all across the world, he seemed effortlessly to cross then well-nigh impenetrable barriers of class, religion, culture and race. Wrench was Protean, while remaining entirely true to himself – because his character was Protean. Born a late nineteenth-century Victorian, he also belonged to the twentieth century and the twenty-first ... and perhaps even beyond.

Starting in the 1920s with the Walter Hines Page award, the ESU initiated a series of undergraduate and postgraduate scholarships. All of these had the same aim: to give the recipient exposure to a different culture and environment, at a formative stage in their lives. They would have an opportunity to 'see the other fellow's point of view'. They would learn to step outside their comfort zones. And they would thereby develop. Selection on merit made it statistically likely that recipients would become future leaders; and so it has proved, with luminaries such as Madame Fu Ying and Sir John Bond. Thus the 'multiplier effect'. You do not give a man a fish to feed him for a day; nor do you simply teach a man to fish so that he can feed himself for a lifetime. *Instead you teach teachers to fish.* Through simple gratitude (as evinced so clearly in 'The Alumnus Experience') those whom you help will tend to support future programmes. Through their leadership – and enhanced personal qualities – they will profoundly affect the lives of untold others. Thus the benefits are vastly multiplied.

Wrench nursed the ESU through the first two decades of its life. Always taking care that it was no one-man-band, no private fiefdom, guiding, occasionally cajoling, always coping with what must have been a remorseless grind of hard work, with *The Landmark*, with committees, with worldwide correspondence tumbling through his letterbox, demanding urgent replies.

We have seen how the role of the ESU changed in the Second World War – firstly to an aid organisation and secondly to a hospitality organisation. Some few names from that era survive: Phyllis Biscoe, Alice Gardiner, Beatrice Warde, Alicia Street. Following the war, Lillian Moore and Yvonne Theobald arrived to renew the educational programmes. The unrivalled contemporary expertise which the ESU has in running educational and cultural programmes owes much to the expertise – and devotion – of these two ladies. Happily, at the time of writing, Alicia Street and Yvonne Theobald are enjoying well-deserved retirements, in Bristol and London respectively. Back in 1920, an early edition of *The Landmark* raised the question, 'Does the ESU allow women?' Delightedly Evelyn Wrench assured everyone that they were more than welcome. Women have flourished in the ESU.

The last great historical spasm of the twentieth century was the 1989 collapse of the Berlin Wall and the dissolution of the Soviet Empire. We have seen how Baroness Brigstocke and Valerie Mitchell capitalised on an opportunity unique in world history. It is often claimed that football management is the most brutal form of the art, a revolving door where you are only as good as your last win. In football management terms, it is as though Valerie Mitchell led teams that won every imaginable title. Appropriately, The President of the English-Speaking Union, HRH The Duke of Edinburgh, presented her with the coveted Churchill Medal of Honour for outstanding services to the ESU and its International Development.

In brief, this is where the ESU has been. Should anyone say 'What does it do? What are the benefits?' we would respectfully direct them to 'The Alumnus Experience'. In short: *ESU programmes transform peoples' lives.* Today's ESU students become tomorrow's international leaders in their chosen disciplines. It would be an interesting exercise to compute how much money has been administered by the ESU over the last ninety years and calculate its worth in present-day terms. It is probable that a single alumnus of the order of Sir John Bond has generated enough money to justify this investment a hundredfold. And Sir John would doubtless be the first to point out that he is one of many thousands of alumni who have repaid their career investments in innumerable ways – economic, cultural, social and educational. ESU alumni become 'multipliers', transforming untold other lives. The ESU has more than ninety years of unrivalled experience and expertise in what it does.

The 1989 collapse of the Berlin Wall was the last great historical spasm of the twentieth century. The first great historical spasm of the twenty-first was the 2001 terrorist attack on the Twin Towers in New York (popularly known as 9/11). As with the 1963 assassination of President Kennedy, the whole world was plunged into shock. People will always remember where they were when they first saw the dreadful images. Michael Ward, a researcher for this book, was about to attempt the hardest rock-climb of his life, one where failure would have involved serious, perhaps fatal injury. When the terrible images from New York came through on a portable television, it was impossible to retain any sense of personal importance. In the face of such carnage, ambition withered. Although he continued to climb that afternoon, it was in search of healing, not achievement. In country after country, all around the globe, people tried to come to terms with the morally incomprehensible.

Almost ten years after 9/11, its grim shadow remains with us, a stark warning to the future of the human race. Can good possibly come out of such a horrible event? The outpouring of humanity in New York and elsewhere was a salutary reminder of the sanctity of human life – all human life. It was as though the materialistic scales had fallen from our eyes and we were in touch with something of fundamental importance which we had been in danger of losing.

The perpetrators of 9/11 would attempt to justify the atrocity as a form of conflict resolution. If war is diplomacy by other means, then assuredly terrorism is war by other means. History attests that short-term gains are unlikely to endure. Certainly history attests that the state-induced terrorism of fascist nations fails to endure. It seems that terrorism carries the seeds of its own downfall. It inspires moral revulsion within all of us.

Undeniably, however, we are in grave need of conflict resolution. Tribalism represents perhaps the simplest and oldest form of human organisation. The power of tribalism is that it works – and, within tribes, it can work very effectively indeed. Yet tribalism practically guarantees tribal conflict – whether ethnic, religious, political or social. The human race has lived with chemical weapons since the First World War. It has lived with atomic weapons since the end of the Second World War. Tribalism and nuclear weapons emphatically do not mix. Consequently, if we do not morally grow up, we will never reach the end of the twenty-first century, for we will have destroyed our planet.

The irony is that most people want what most people have always wanted – peace, a decent standard of living, a chance to bring up their families in security. We don't need to be professional historians to know that fascism doesn't work, communism doesn't work, rabid fundamentalism doesn't work and robber baron capitalism doesn't work. All of these are repressive; and what inspires repression simply does not work.

Democracy, political moderation and social tolerance seem to hold the best hopes for the human race. Do these values seem familiar? Well they should do ... for they were the values of John Evelyn Wrench.

And what about conflict resolution? Well Wrench was the man who could always see the other fellow's point of view. He was the man who always remained on good terms with everyone else, while remaining absolutely true to his own publicly declared beliefs. Crucially Wrench realised that, in practice, tolerance is not best learned in an ivory tower. It is best learned through exposure to other races, other cultures and other belief systems. Let us recall that passage about his early life: 'As a boy I was taken on some of my father's tours of inspection. I have vivid recollections of thirty or forty mile drives in outlying parts of Connemara, away from railways, seated sideways on an Irish car in drenching rain, wrapped up in a tarpaulin ...' Courtesy of his father, Wrench was meeting people from a different religion and a vastly different social class, with sharply differing political beliefs. Conflict resolution? *He was living it, day in and day out.* Those early lessons stood him in good stead, with his teenage travels to Europe, Russia and Asia and his adult travels to Canada, America, Australia, South Africa and elsewhere.

The Future of the English-Speaking Union

The first edition of *The Landmark* expressed the intention that the ESU would link up the sheep farmer in Australia with the New York businessman, and the gold miner in South Africa with the fruit grower in California. Why? Because Wrench knew that their commonality was far greater than their differences and that the future of the world depended upon such commonality.

The Walter Hines Page Scholarship launched a plethora of ESU scholarships, all with the same aim of transforming lives via exposure to novel environments. Why? Because Wrench knew that this is what works. And if you pick 'multipliers', the likely leaders of tomorrow, your return on investment is enormous.

So many charities are formed by messianic visionaries only to find, in later years, the world has changed to such a degree that the original vision has become sadly redundant. Such organisations often struggle to reposition themselves. However, in the sage words of the ESU's long-standing President, HRH The Duke of Edinburgh: 'The great thing about Sir Evelyn Wrench's idea is that it was relevant at the time it was conceived and it has remained relevant ever since.'

Not only has the idea remained relevant – it has become immeasurably *more* relevant than ever before. Why? There are two reasons. The first reason is that the world has freely chosen globalisation. And the second reason is that the world has freely chosen English to be its global language. The language of rock music, movies, the internet, scientific discourse, international business, and so much else, is English. Billions of people want globalisation – and billions of people want English.

Where does this leave the English-Speaking Union? Robert Service's *Law of the Yukon*, originally written as a paean to nineteenth-century gold prospectors, applies equally to twenty-first century charities:

> This is the Law of the Yukon, that only the Strong shall thrive;
> That surely the Weak shall perish, and only the Fit survive.

The paradox is this: while a charity may dispense largesse, it cannot depend upon largesse. In today's economic climate, a non-profit making organisation needs to be as well positioned in its 'market', as efficient in its operations and as cost-effective as any commercial organisation. But – and this is crucial – it must also embody a highly distinctive ethos and culture which says: this is what we do (and this is what we do not do), this is how we do it and, above all, this is why it matters.

Does the ESU give value to its sponsors, whether that sponsor be a multinational or a branch member? Undoubtedly it does. A sponsor will be rewarded with delightful social gatherings with a variety of interesting people from all walks of life. Always the sponsor knows that there is a serious purpose behind every gathering, no matter how enjoyable. 'Creating global understanding through English' is achieved through transforming peoples' lives and knowing that many of these people will go on to transform innumerable other lives. Every £1 spent with the ESU will repay investment again and again.

As we have seen, in the last twenty years ESU 'market penetration' of world countries has increased from 7% to 28% – beyond the wildest dreams of any professional marketer. Amazingly this has happened through 'the countries coming to us ... We were there for them.' Is this astounding result a defiance of conventional marketing? Well, in some ways it is. Certainly it stands in defiance of the slickness of so much conventional marketing – a slickness with which we're getting heartily tired – especially when often accompanied by poor operational delivery. (With over ninety years of expertise in what it does, the ESU's operational delivery is practically guaranteed to be extremely good.)

But there is a more important factor at work. That marketing genius, the late Gary Halbert, was once asked what was the best marketing device of all. He replied that the best marketing device of all was no technique, no gimmick; rather it was the positioning of your product or service in front of 'a hungry crowd', i.e. a market which was clamouring for it. Over the last twenty years, this is exactly what the ESU has done. Helping country after country enhance their 'cultural passports', giving them an entrée on to the world stage, is positioning yourself in front of a crowd which is not merely hungry but ravenous.

Today acquiring a 'cultural passport' is essential for the economic survival of all countries. Such a 'cultural passport' involves immeasurably more than merely speaking English. It means an understanding of other countries, other cultures, other *mores*, other ways of business and social life. Above all it involves the same 'tolerance of ambiguity' that Sir Evelyn Wrench symbolises. You have to learn to interact with people who may be very different from yourself. You have to find commonality with them. No country in the world can afford to close its doors. We need each other too much. Jean Monnet's 'interdependence' has become reality for our global village.

Of course it is essential that each country preserves its languages, its dialects, its history and its culture. The last thing we want is everywhere getting like everywhere else. Niche tourists, such as hikers, skiers, climbers and scuba divers demand difference – that's why they come. And niche tourism (which has the highest rate of repeat business) is becoming ever more important. Preserving distinctiveness is essential – not just for tourism but, more importantly, for the welfare of the inhabitants. Each country must preserve its individual identity. The 'cultural passport' is Janus-faced – a portal to the world *and* a means of preserving national identity.

Countries need to market themselves; so too do regions, communities, organisations and individuals. Use English and your message will be heard by dozens, hundreds, perhaps even thousands of times more people. The better you employ the language, the better you will get your point of view across. The world cannot afford 9/11 'conflict resolution'. It is morally abhorrent, it pursues short-term gains at the direct expense of genuine conflict resolution and – most terrifying of all – it is a madness which, if unchecked, will lead to the destruction of us all. In the twenty-first century, we *must* change. We *must* morally grow up. We *must* deal with ambiguity. We *must* 'see the other fellow's point of view'. We *must* learn to communicate superbly. We *must* celebrate interdependence.

Today, in the UK, home of the world's oldest democracy, there are schools where, shockingly, pupils attempt to resolve conflict with knives, where guns are not far away. In these circumstances, conflict is not resolved; instead it is perpetuated. Irrespective of personal religious belief (or its absence) the wise Biblical comment about the sins of the fathers being visited upon successive generations instils a dreadful warning. Spirals of violence, if unchecked, merely perpetuate ever-greater spirals of violence.

It is illuminating talking with ESU staff members who have gone into inner city schools of dire deprivation, which had nevertheless not been 'written off' by their head-teachers. When pupils learn to express themselves, to get their points of view across, to debate, to reach consensus, then they learn genuine conflict resolution. And genuine conflict resolution is essential for the future of our planet.

So many organisations struggle for a USP – a Unique Specific Proposition, a distinctiveness, a reason to stand out from the crowd. The ESU has unequalled prowess in transforming peoples' lives and thereby creating global understanding through English.

There is a simple litmus test of any organisation – walk through the front door of its head-office. You will quickly get a very strong sense of the values of the organisation. Are people officious or courteous? Are they distant or friendly? Are they rude or polite? *Do they care about what they are doing?*

Walk through the door of Dartmouth House and you will feel the difference. You will be in a world of convivial people who care deeply about what they are doing. Have lunch in the exquisite Revelstoke Room, under the benevolent eye of Dr Walter Hines Page. Wander into the courtyard and muse on the commemoration to Evelyn Wrench. It could not be more simple, more direct, more artless.

What Others
Have Dreamed
He Has Done

Dartmouth House resonates with the twin spirits of Dr Walter Hines Page and Sir John Evelyn Wrench. It resonates with the spirits of generations of staff and volunteers, many of them now unknown, who gave decades of their lives to the work of the English-Speaking Union. When you open the front door of Dartmouth House, there is the strangest sense of coming home.

The efforts of the last ninety years have culminated in the establishment of a highly enviable network of ESUs across the world. The ESU has an infrastructure to rival any multinational. It has unrivalled expertise in what it does. The future of the English-Speaking Union is surely to build upon that infrastructure and to deploy the power of its network of ESUs for maximum mutual benefit. The world desperately needs to manage change – and the English-Speaking Union is a crucial catalyst of such change. In the words of Valerie Mitchell:

> The nature of nationhood is being re-examined and communications led by the English language are breaking down traditional barriers throughout the globe. The English-Speaking Union is at the forefront of this movement and consequently is undergoing a momentous period in its history. It has risen to the occasion and recognised the great contribution it is able to make on the world stage.
>
> The world as always is in the midst of troubled times and difficulties, however dire, have a silver lining. The English-Speaking Union is that silver lining.

Evelyn Wrench was one of a small band of intrepid Victorians who were light years ahead of their time. Queen Victoria herself, despite tragedy and ill-health, bequeathed a model of constitutional monarchy as the staunchest possible defence of democracy. Prince Albert was a socially inspired polymath. To take but one example of his consummate ability; his Great Exhibition, at Crystal Palace, is the template for every convention, every trade fair, every exhibition in the world today, from Frankfurt Book Fair to Silicon Valley. Their daughter, Princess Alice, was an inspired nurse and social reformer, a shining practical example of how privilege may be used to transform lives. Her close friend, Florence Nightingale, another polymath, created the profession of nursing and attained standards of patient care which, over a century later, have never been bettered.

And Evelyn Wrench? He knew that we had to learn to understand difference. He knew that we had to learn to resolve conflict. He knew that we had to reach out beyond racial, cultural, social barriers and say, *'This man is my brother. This woman is my sister.'*

Over the last ninety years, the English-Speaking Union has helped to transform so many thousands of lives. Now, in the second decade of the twenty-first century, there is much more that must be done. Ever onward!

Appendices

APPENDIX I

The commemoration to Sir John Evelyn Wrench at Dartmouth House, headquarters of the English-Speaking Union.

To Recognise
And Record
The Work Of
John Evelyn
Wrench
Companion of the Order
Of St Michael and St George
As Founder
Of The English
Speaking Union
What Others
Have Dreamed
He Has Done

APPENDIX II

On 28 June 1918 Evelyn Wrench invited fifteen friends to dine with him at the Marlborough Club, in London to discuss the formation of the English-Speaking Union. The fifteen friends were:

Sir Algernon Aspinall

Mr Boylston Beal (USA), Secretary to Dr Walter Hines Page

Major Ian Hay Beith

Mr John Buchan, the novelist, later Lord Tweedsmuir

Professor McNeil Dixon

The Revd W. F. Geikie-Cobb

Sir Arthur Herbert

Mr Francis Jones

Mr James Keeley (USA)

Sir George Mills McKay

Mr Henry Noyes (Australia)

Mr Francis E. Powell (USA), Chairman of the American Chamber of Commerce

Mr A. Lyle Samuel

Sir George Sutton, Chairman of the Amalgamated Press

Mr Fullerton Waldo (USA), an executive of the *Philadelphia Ledger*

APPENDIX III

As of the time of writing, the following countries have joined the English-Speaking Union:

United States of America	1920
Australia	1922
Bermuda	1922
Canada	1923
New Zealand	1924
Scotland	1952
Pakistan	1961
Belgium	1975
Nigeria	1980
Sri Lanka	1981
Germany	1982
India	1984
France	1987
Austria	1989
Finland	1991
Hungary	1991
Serbia	1991
Sierra Leone	1991
Bulgaria	1992
Denmark	1992
Argentina	1993
Mauritius	1993
Nepal	1993

Poland	1993
Portugal	1994
Lithuania	1996
Romania	1996
Japan	1998
Armenia	1998
Latvia	1998
Russia	1998
Vanuatu	1998
Brazil	1999
Morocco	2000
Hong Kong	2001
Thailand	2001
Georgia	2002
Malaysia	2002
Lebanon	2003
Madagascar	2003
Mongolia	2003
South Korea	2004
Chile	2005
Czech Republic	2005
Mexico	2005
Philippines	2005
Moldova	2007
Estonia	2008
Albania	2009
Cyprus	2009
Bangladesh	2010
Malta	2010
Turkey	2010

APPENDIX IV

As of the time of writing, the following English-Speaking Union regions and branches exist within the UK:

NORTH EAST REGION

Northumberland and Durham
Lincolnshire
York and District

NORTH WEST REGION

Chester
Liverpool and Merseyside
Mid-Cheshire (formerly Vale Royal Cheshire)
Manchester and East Cheshire
Shropshire

MIDLANDS REGION

Birmingham
Derby and Nottingham
Gloucestershire
Herefordshire
Oxfordshire
Worcestershire

WALES REGION

Appendix IV

LONDON REGION

EAST REGION

Cambridge Welland Valley (formerly East Midlands)
Colchester
Epping Forest (formerly Metropolitan Essex)
Hertfordshire
Norwich and Norfolk
Ouse Valley
Southend-on-Sea
Suffolk

SOUTH REGION

Salisbury and South Wilts

SOUTH EAST REGION

Brighton, Hove and District
Canterbury and East Kent
Eastbourne
Guildford and District
1066 (formerly Hastings)
Tunbridge Wells
West Sussex

SOUTH WEST REGION

Bath and District
Bristol
Cornwall
Exeter and District
Plymouth and District
Taunton and District

APPENDIX V

The English-Speaking Union Patron

1952–	HM Queen Elizabeth II

APPENDIX VI

The English-Speaking Union

Presidents

1918–30	The Lord Balfour, KG
1930–33	The Rt. Hon. Viscount Grey of Fallodon, KG
1934–35	HRH The Prince of Wales, KG
1937–41	The Marquess of Wellington, PC, GCSI, GCMG, GCIE, GBE
1943–51	The Rt. Hon. The Lord Cranborne, KG
1951–52	HRH The Princess Elizabeth, Duchess of Edinburgh
1952–	HRH The Prince Philip, Duke of Edinburgh, KG, KT

APPENDIX VII

The English-Speaking Union

Chairmen

1918–19	Evelyn Wrench, CMG
1920–21	The Lord Reading, PC, GCB, GCSI, GCIE, GCVO
1921–25	The Rt. Hon. Winston Churchill, CH
1926–35	The Marquess of Reading, PC, GCB, GCSI, GCIE, GCVO
1936–37	The Marquess of Willingdon, PC, GCSI, GCMG, GCIE, GBE
1937–43	Sir Evelyn Wrench, CMG
1943–46	Dame Edith Lyttelton, GBE
1946–51	The Rt. Hon. The Lord Wakehurst, KCMG
1951–64	The Lord Baillieu, KBE, CMG
1964–68	Sir Basil Smallpiece, KCVO
1969–72	Sir John Benn
1973–83	Sir Patrick Dean, GCMG
1983–87	Sir Donald Tebbit, GCMG
1987–92	The Rt. Hon. The Lord Pym, MC
1992–93	Lady Luce (Acting)
1993–99	The Baroness Brigstocke
1999–2005	The Lord Watson of Richmond, CBE
2005–	The Rt. Hon. The Lord Hunt of Wirral, MBE, PC

APPENDIX VIII

The English-Speaking Union

Directors-General

The post was created as a result of Lady Reading's report on ESU reorganisation. The original brief was 'to be in charge of all the activities of the Union and to co-ordinate the work of the various departments'.

1938–39 Sir Frederick Whyte, KCSI (At the outbreak of the Second World War, Sir Frederick joined the Ministry of Information and the post lapsed.)

1947–49 Air Chief Marshal Sir Douglas Evill, GBE, KCB, DSC, AFC

1949–57 Mr Frank Darvall

1957–64 Air Chief Marshal Sir Francis Fogarty, GBE, KCB, DFC, AFC

1964–68 Morris Barr

1970–73 Kathleen M. Graham, CBE
(The post was renamed 'Executive Director'. Kathleen Graham subsequently became Director of International Affairs.)

1973–77 W. N. Hugh Jones, MVO, MA

1977–79 Major-General David C. Alexander, CB

1979–87 Alan Lee Williams, OBE

1987–90 Rear Admiral Richard Heaslip, CB

1990–91 David Hicks, MBE
Previously Deputy Director-General, c. 1985

1991–94 David Thorpe

1994–2009	Valerie Mitchell, OBE (previously Deputy Director-General, 1990–94)
2010–	Mike Lake, CBE

Select Bibliography

Correspondence between HRH The Prince Philip, Duke of Edinburgh and the English-Speaking Union (1952–2010), Buckingham Palace, London

Journals of the English-Speaking Union, 1918–2010
Jones, Hugh, *Campaigning Face to Face*, Sussex, 2007
Watson, Alan, *Jamestown, The Voyage of English*, London, 2007
Wrench, John Evelyn, *Uphill: The First Stage of a Strenuous Life*, London, 1934
Wrench, John Evelyn, *Struggle, 1914–1920*, London, 1935

Index

Please note that officers of the ESU are listed in the Appendices; also UK regional branches and ESU members overseas